YOU ARE
THE UMPIRE

An Hachette UK Company
www.hachette.co.uk

First published in Great Britain in 2019
by Cassell, an imprint of Octopus Publishing
Group Ltd
Carmelite House, 50 Victoria Embankment
London EC4Y 0DZ
www.octopusbooks.co.uk

ISBN 978-0-60063-574-1

A CIP catalogue record for this book is
available from the British Library.

The views expressed in the book are those
of the Author and not the Publisher.

Printed and bound in China
10 9 8 7 6 5 4 3 2 1

Project Editor: Cathy Meeus
Designer: Hugh Schermuly

Publishing Director: Trevor Davies
Editor: Ella Parsons
Art Director: Juliette Norsworthy
Senior Production Manager: Peter Hunt

YOU ARE THE UMPIRE

300 cricketing conundrums for you to solve

Paul Trevillion & John Holder

The Umpire

Foreword

Michael Holding

Cricket is such a marvellous game. I have thoroughly enjoyed the years that I played and am now enjoying the years of making a living talking about this great game. Cricket is unique in many ways and I have found – even after being involved in the sport for so many years – there are still things to be learned about the game, including elements of the laws and playing conditions. The playing conditions have always varied depending on the combatants and where the combats have taken place, but the laws have varied little... and yet we continue to learn more and more about them.

I am glad to know that John has written a book to help the layman and woman – and to be honest even us paid pundits – understand the laws and explain exactly what an umpire can and cannot do under various circumstances. John played the game for many years before embarking on another long career umpiring and coaching both young players and umpires, so he is extremely well qualified to write such a book.

I hope everyone enjoys reading *You Are the Umpire* and I know that in doing so they will have a greater understanding of the laws of this great game.

Mikey.

Umpiring signals

Signalling is an essential part of the umpire's role. Making the standard signals clearly enables the players, spectators and scorers to understand what has happened on the field of play.

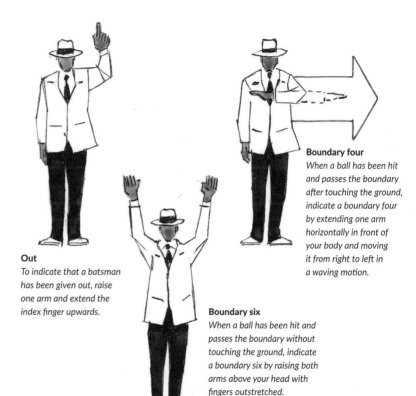

Out
To indicate that a batsman has been given out, raise one arm and extend the index finger upwards.

Boundary four
When a ball has been hit and passes the boundary after touching the ground, indicate a boundary four by extending one arm horizontally in front of your body and moving it from right to left in a waving motion.

Boundary six
When a ball has been hit and passes the boundary without touching the ground, indicate a boundary six by raising both arms above your head with fingers outstretched.

Bye

When a legitimate ball passes the striking batsman without touching the batsman's bat or body and the batsman scores one or more runs, indicate a bye by extending one arm vertically with fingers outstretched.

No ball

If the bowler delivers a ball from the wrong place, if the ball bounces more than twice or it rolls, or if the delivery is deemed to be dangerous, indicate a no ball by extending one arm horizontally at a right angle to your body with fingers outstretched. Call out 'no ball'.

Dead ball

In any circumstance where you deem the ball no longer to be in play, indicate dead ball by bending forwards while extending your arms downwards and repeatedly crossing them in front of your body. Call out 'dead ball'.

Leg byes

When a legitimate ball does not touch the bat, but (providing there is no leg before wicket) strikes the body of the batsman, who then scores one or more runs, indicate a leg bye by raising one leg and tapping the raised leg repeatedly with one hand.

Wide ball

If you judge that the batsman did not have a fair chance to hit the ball, you may indicate a wide ball. Extend both arms simultaneously at right angles from your body with fingers outstretched and call out 'wide ball'.

Short run

When a batsman fails to ground the bat behind the crease on completion of a run, rule a short run by using one arm to repeatedly pat the top of the shoulder on the same side. Call out 'short run'.

Revoke the last signal

The umpire may cancel a decision after consultation with another on-field umpire or a television umpire by crossing both arms across the chest with the palms of the hands on opposite shoulders. You may recall the batsman verbally, then make the revoke signal to the scorers.

Five penalty runs

Either team can be awarded five penalty runs for specific offences. To award the batting side, repeatedly pat your shoulder with the opposite hand. To award the fielding side, rest your hand on the opposite shoulder.

LEVEL 3

LEVEL 4

Sending a player off for bad behaviour

There are four levels of bad behaviour, with Level 3 and Level 4 being the most serious. For a Level 3 offence, where a player is being sent off for a specific period of overs only, the umpire facing the scorers at the bowler's end repeatedly raises and lowers an arm outstretched to shoulder height. He raises the other arm vertically, with the number of fingers outstretched to indicate how many overs the ban will last. For a Level 4 offence, the bowler's end umpire raises one arm outstretched horizontally to shoulder height and raises the other arm vertically with the index finger oustretched. This means that the player has been sent off for the remainder of the match.

Key changes to the laws of cricket

The first Laws of Cricket were codified in 1744 (although the earliest printed account is from 1755) by members of the London Cricket Club. It set out many of the core elements of the game, including the height of the stumps, no balls and fielders having to appeal for a player to be out. It did, however, say an over should last four balls. This was changed to five in 1889 and finally to six in 1900 (although this wasn't adopted universally until 1979).

The Marylebone Cricket Club (MCC) has been the custodian of the Laws since its creation in 1787. Over the years there have been seven recoding of the Laws of Cricket, with the latest being released in October 2017. Here are the key changes:

1. The 'Handled the Ball' law has been removed and merged with 'Obstructing the Field'.

2. The striker can be caught from a ball that comes off the bat and deflects off the helmet of the wicketkeeper or a fielder.

3. The striker can be caught if a ball becomes lodged in the visor of the wicketkeeper's or a fielder's helmet.

4. The striker can be run out from a ball that rebounds off any fielder's helmet and breaks the wicket.

5. Play must be suspended if one umpire considers playing conditions to be dangerous. When off the field, both umpires must agree for play to start or restart.

6. Umpires have the power to have a player sent off the field of play. The relevant captain will be told to send his player off. Failure to do so will result in the match being forfeited.

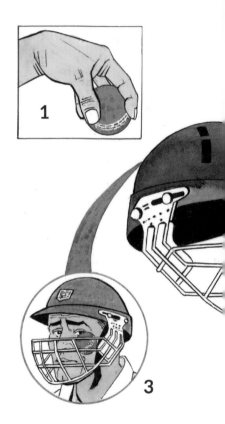

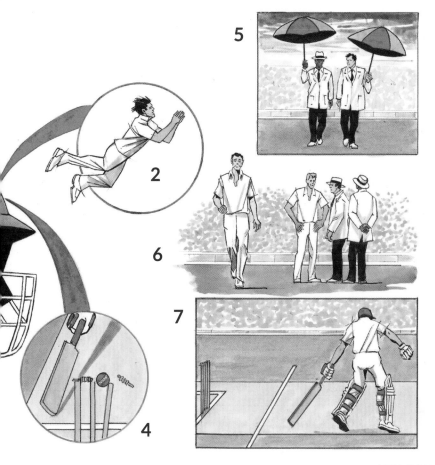

7. In the case of deliberate short runs, both batsmen will be returned to their original ends and the runs will not count. Five penalty runs will be awarded to the fielding side and both players reported. That ball will not count in the over.

8. The 'Lost Ball' law has been removed. In the rare situations where this may arise, the 'Dead Ball' law will apply.

9. There is now one warning given to a player for damaging the pitch.

10. The law preventing a fielder from deliberately deceiving or distracting a batsman – for example, by chasing the ball and pretending to have stopped it – has been clarified and strengthened.

11. A new law penalises the bowler for deliberately overstepping the popping crease.

12. A striker cannot take guard on the Protected Area (previously called the Danger Area).

Giving LBW

Sixty per cent of all decisions made by umpires involve LBW but for umpires, giving LBW is the most difficult decision of all because it is a matter of opinion whether or not the ball would have hit the wicket. Nevertheless, the bowler's end umpire is in the best position to make that judgement.

The decision has to be made in conditions that are often highly pressurised. The crowd is raucous, the fielding team are shouting and the bowler is almost on bended knees pleading for you to raise your finger. Despite all these distractions you have to make a decision on a moment in time that could have lasted less than a second based on the following considerations:

- Was it a legal delivery?
- Would the ball have hit the wicket?
- Where did the ball pitch?
- If outside the line of the off stump, was the striker playing a shot?
- Did the striker edge the ball?
- Was the ball delivered from close to the wicket or wide on the crease?
- How far down the pitch was the striker?
- How tall was the striker?
- How far did the ball have to travel to hit the wicket?
- How much was the ball swinging, moving or turning?
- Was the bounce high or low?

Obtaining an accurate view

The umpire stands at a distance from the wicket, from where he can clearly see if the bowler's front foot lands behind or over the back edge of the popping crease. The umpire must then raise his eyes to pick up the ball in flight. It is essential that the head of the umpire is kept as still as possible in order to be able to pick up the ball in flight. The faster the bowler, the more crucial this is. Should there be an appeal, the umpire must carefully weigh up all the elements, then make a decision. It is imperative that aggressive appealing from players does not influence the decision.

The following are key considerations when adjudicating on an LBW appeal:

Off stump

- If the batsman is hit on the pads outside the line of the off stump while playing a stroke, you cannot give out LBW even if you judge the ball would have gone on to hit the wicket.
- If the batsman is hit on the pads outside the line of the off stump offering no stroke, you can give out if you judge the ball would have gone on to hit the wicket.

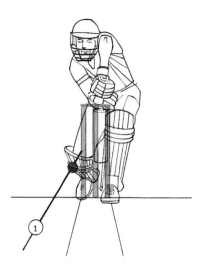

Outside leg stump

To reduce the chances of dismissal in this manner, the lawmakers have decided that a batsman cannot be given out LBW to a ball pitching outside the line of the leg stump. It was felt that batting was perilous enough with all the other ways of dismissal.

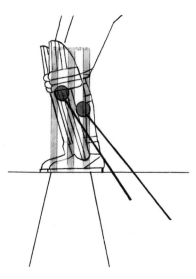

On the fourth day of an Ashes Test at Old Trafford, Australia, who were bowling, were desperate for a wicket as England strolled towards victory. Shane Warne went around the wicket to Freddie Flintoff, pitching and sharply turning a ball into the rough outside Flintoff's leg stump. Flintoff raised his bat high, turned his body and placed his pads in front of the wicket. The ball cannoned into his pads. All eleven Aussies appealed but the umpire ruled not out. Hawk-Eye showed that the ball would have hit middle stump. Why was Flintoff not given out?

The anwer is that the batsman cannot be given out LBW to any ball that pitches outside the leg stump.

Angle of delivery

There are a few reasons why seam bowlers especially strive to bowl wicket to wicket. The wicket is only nine inches wide and delivering from close to the wicket and bowling straight at the striker's wicket boosts the chances of bowling the striker and getting LBWs should the striker miss (1). What's more, with slip fielders in place, the ball only has to move away slightly to clip the edge of the bat and get the striker caught at slip.

The wider of the wicket the ball pitches (2), the less of the wicket it is likely to hit. This means there's a greater chance of missing the wicket on either leg or off.

The former Australian fast bowler Terry Alderman bowled from closer to the wicket than any other seam bowler I have ever known. As a result, a high proportion of his wickets were LBW, bowled and caught at slip. John Emburey, the former Middlesex and England off spinner, bowled from even closer than Alderman. Many of his victims were bowled and LBW. It is a matter of angles.

- The bowler who stands close to the wicket when delivering the ball has a straighter angle to the stumps.
- The bowler who stands wide on the popping crease has a much wider angle of delivery, which creates added doubt if the ball would have passed outside the leg stump.

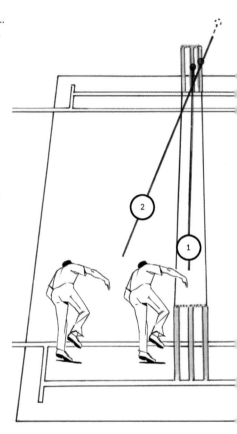

Fair delivery

In a situation where you've established that if there was no bat involved, the ball would have hit the stumps, and would have pitched either in line or on off, you now have to confirm that it was a fair delivery. It is a legal delivery if the bowler's front foot is behind the popping crease (see below).

If in delivery any part of the bowler's back foot touches or lands outside the line of the return crease, the bowler's end umpire will immediately call and signal no ball. This isn't an easy thing to pick up when all the action is some 20 yards away.

In a county match, the away team's third wicket pair batted well, putting on 180 runs. In desperation, the opposition took the second new ball. The striker played back off the first ball, but the ball skidded through and hit his pad. Although the delivery looked good, the umpire called and signalled no ball.

TV replays showed that the back of the bowler's heel was resting on the popping crease and that no part of his foot was behind the line. It should be noted that the back edge of the popping crease is the crease.

The grass was slightly wet before a match, but play started on time. The opening bowler raced in, landed behind the popping crease, but his foot slid about a foot over the line. The striker was bowled, but his colleague claimed that the delivery was a no ball. He was wrong. The law says the important consideration is where the foot lands, not where it finally ends up. It would be grossly unfair to penalise a bowler whose foot slipped on landing.

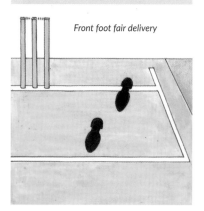
Front foot no ball delivery

Front foot fair delivery

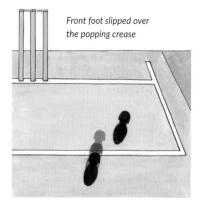
Front foot slipped over the popping crease

Review and referral systems

The referral and review systems arose as a result of televised cricket, and the former has been in operation for about 30 years. In an effort to reduce umpire errors, the International Cricket Council (ICC) brought in the Decision Review System (DRS) in 2009.

Referral

A referral may be requested by the on-field umpires for specific decisions in response to an appeal, the validity of which they are unsure. Decisions that may be referred are:

- Run out
- Stumping
- Clean catches
- Hit wicket
- Boundary fielding

The television umpire makes a final decision, which is then displayed on the replay screen on the ground.

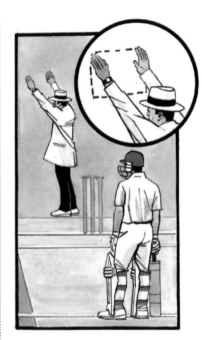

To call for a review, the umpire makes the shape of a television to his television umpiring colleagues.

Review

A review is triggered by a challenge to the umpire's decision by the batsmen at the crease or the fielding captain and must be made within 15 seconds of the umpire's decision. The television umpire reviews all available video footage from high-resolution cameras, Snicko and Hot Spot, then advises the on-field umpire either to stay with his original decision or to change it. A review can last 3–4 minutes.

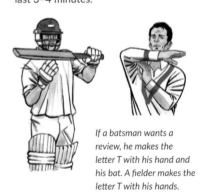

If a batsman wants a review, he makes the letter T with his hand and his bat. A fielder makes the letter T with his hands.

LBW reviewed

Umpires should only give a batsman out if he is certain that the batsman is out. But because LBW is a matter of opinion, not fact, there is an added element of difficulty. Umpires give the benefit of doubt when assessing whether the ball was likely to hit the outer edge of the wicket.

Hawk-Eye, the computerised system used for assessing the trajectory of a ball, is said to be more accurate than any umpire in predicting the path of the ball if it had not been intercepted. But not even Hawk-Eye can be said to be 100 per cent accurate, so the umpire's call comes into play.

The following scenario is an example of how television technology is used. The West Indies fast bowler Kemar Roach sends down a good length ball to Joe Root, who goes forward to play a defensive shot. The ball thuds into his front pad. There is an appeal. The umpire gives Root out LBW. After conferring with his colleague, Root makes the signal asking for a review. The television umpire checks the front foot to ensure the delivery was legal. If it isn't, there's no need to go any further – he is not out. The delivery was good so he turns to the Hot Spot and Snicko technology to confirm that the ball did not make contact with the bat. The final check is ball-tracking to determine where on the pads the ball struck and if the ball would have hit the wicket. The review showed that the ball would have hit the wicket but struck the pad outside the line of the off stump. Because he was playing a stroke, Root could not be given out LBW.

In 1995 I was the television umpire in the Edgbaston Test between England and the West Indies. The visitors batted only once, winning the match before lunch on the third day. During the match, there was a run out incident, which could only have been spotted by television replay technology.

West Indies pace bowler Kenny Benjamin went for a sharp run towards the pavilion end. The wicket was broken with Benjamin struggling to make his ground. Umpire Peter Willey signalled to me that he wanted a referral, whereupon I asked the television director to start the

Run out reviewed

In the case of a run out, with a batsman running at 14mph and inches from the popping crease, the movement of the bat is a blur, but with the use of super slow-motion cameras, it is possible to see exactly where the bat is at the moment the wicket is broken. Relying on only the naked eye, the decision would be pure guesswork and the umpire would be likely to rule not out.

slow-motion replay process. It was difficult to be absolutely decisive until I asked to rock the camera back and forth. Only then was it clear that the bat was on the crease when the wicket was broken. The director then displayed 'out' on the giant screen and Benjamin left the field.

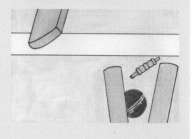

THE QUESTIONS

In a one-day match, the opening fast bowler skittles the first three batsmen. The opposing captain decides on a change in his batting order. The hurried reshuffle means the next batsman has taken longer than three minutes to walk to the crease. The fielding side appeal for the batsman to be timed out. What is your decision?

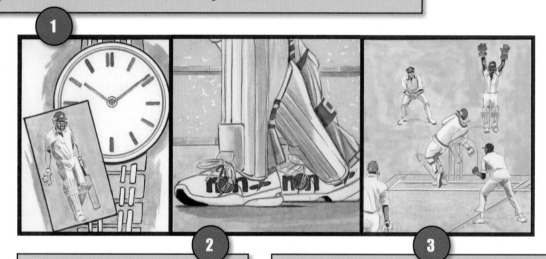

1

2

A batsman whose run-scoring feats have made him a box-office attraction walks to the crease with his new sponsor's name emblazoned on both sides of his cricket boots. Do you take any action?

3

A batsman has just hit his fourth consecutive six. Trying for another six from a slow delivery, his leg-side swipe results only in a thick top edge. The ball pops gently up in the air and, as it falls to the ground, the batsman accidentally catches it with the back of his bat and it is caught. Out or not out?

A fielder, sliding along the ground to stop a four, comes into contact with the boundary rope, pushing it well back. When the fielder gets up, he realises that had the boundary rope not been pushed back, the ball would have made contact, so he throws the ball back to the wicketkeeper and signals a four, but his captain insists it's only three runs – the ball must make contact with the boundary. What is your decision?

6

4

A fielder on the boundary signing autographs suddenly realises the ball has been hit in his direction. He steps back onto the field, inadvertently holding the autograph book. He drops the book on the ground in front of the ball, stopping its forward roll, then throws the ball back to the wicketkeeper. The batsmen have made two runs. What now?

5

A striker deliberately lets a good length ball hit his pad. It deflects onto his bat and then over the keeper. The batsmen run a single, but the fielding captain complains that no stroke was offered, so no runs should be scored. What do you do?

A batsman completes a quick single, but just as his bat slides over the popping crease, the fielder's throw hits his bat and flies off in the opposite direction, allowing the batsman to complete a second run. Does the second run count?

7

The fielding captain points out that the player who has come in for an injured batsman is wearing lightweight running shoes, not standard cricket boots. Do you ask the player to change his footwear?

8

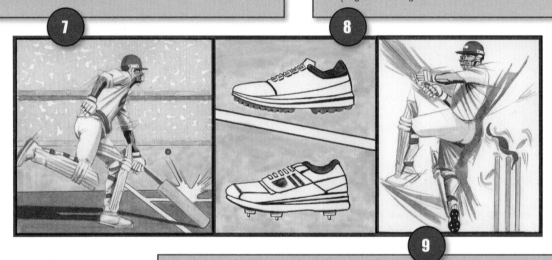

9

It is an exceptionally hot day in a village cricket match. The next batsman in walks to the crease with a large handkerchief tied around his neck which has been soaked in cold water. The batsman hammers the first ball he receives towards the boundary, but before it crosses the boundary rope, the handkerchief, which obviously had not been tied tightly enough, falls off and dislodges the bails. Out or not out?

In a frantic run-chasing Twenty20 match, the home side need four runs off the last two balls in the final over to win. The facing batsman steps out of the crease and hammers the ball, which flies like a bullet straight at the non-striking batsman, who is backing up almost halfway down the wicket. He ducks as he turns his back on the ball, which cannons off his bat and over the boundary ropes. What is your decision?

The wicketkeeper is having a nightmare match, having dropped three straightforward catches. When a fielder goes off injured, he is replaced by a specialist slip fielder, and the fielding captain wants him to take over the gloves. Do you allow this?

A batsman plays a wild drive and actually hits the ball in midair twice while completing his stroke. What action do you take?

The batsman drills the ball straight back along the ground past the bowler. It hits the umpire's boot and rebounds back to the bowler, who picks it up and throws it to spread-eagle the stumps, with the non-striker out of his crease. Out or not out?

13

14

15

Off the last ball of the over, the home batsman completes the run to win the match and raises his bat skywards, acknowledging the crowds riotous applause, but he had not at any time grounded his bat inside the popping crease. Does the run count?

On an extremely hot day, a batsman asks permission to change his shirt at the wicket, pointing out that shirt changes on court are allowed in tennis. What is your decision?

A spin bowler cuts a finger while fumbling a return catch, and needs a plaster. But the batting captain is unhappy: he says the plaster counts as a bowling aid, and the bowler should not be allowed to bowl the last two balls of the over. Do you agree?

16

17

18

Before a game at a leafy ground, it was agreed that the local rule would apply: hitting any overhanging branch counts as a six. But when a fielder's throw back to the wicketkeeper strikes a branch there's confusion all round. Do you award a six, four overthrows or something else?

The square-leg umpire, who recently retired as a player, forgets himself and instinctively takes a catch, throwing the ball jubilantly into the air. Before it lands it is caught by a fielder, who appeals. What now?

A bowler repeatedly breaks the wicket with his knee on delivery. Both batsmen complain that the breaking of the wicket is distracting them. What do you do?

20

19

When a batsman sets off for a quick single, a fielder gathers the ball cleanly and hurls it at the stumps. As the batsman stretches to try to make his ground, the ball hits him on the helmet and cannons into the stumps. Is he out?

21

A batsman hammers a delivery straight back at the non-striking batsman, who instinctively catches it to avoid being hurt. He then hands the ball to the bowler, who appeals for the catch. What now?

A batsman's swipe misses a slow ball, which miraculously lands in his pocket. Thinking quickly, he sprints off over the boundary, without touching the ball with his hands, hoping for a six. What now?

22

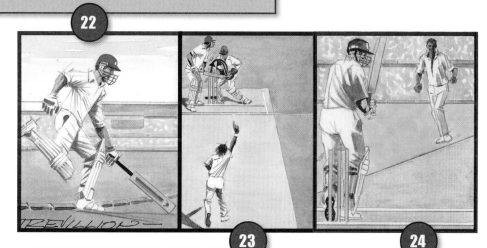

23

A keeper fumbles a catch, which drops onto the bails and bounces back into his hands. The batsman was in his crease so there is no stumping, but the fielding side appeal. Out or not out?

24

A fast bowler has just begun his delivery stride, when the batsman, when stepping back, unfortunately allows his heel to touch the stumps and both bails fall to the ground. The bowler has still not released the ball, but the wicketkeeper appeals. What is your decision?

A fielding team heading for defeat spot dark storm clouds approaching, so start to adopt delaying tactics, hoping for an abandonment. The captain keeps tinkering with the field placing, prompting the opposing team to complain. What do you do?

Two fielders clash heads just as one of them makes a clean catch. The catcher falls down unconscious, still holding the ball. But on impact with the ground the ball comes out of his hand. Has he completed the catch?

As a batsman desperately tries to complete a second run, the wicketkeeper behind him hurls the ball towards his wicket. The batsman changes course and runs into the path of the ball. The fielding side appeal. What is your decision?

A ball is rolling towards the boundary for a certain four, but before it reaches the rope a helpful youngster steps over, picks it up, and tosses it to the chasing fielder. What do you do?

29

28

After a fielding mix-up, the batsmen have already run four by the time a fielder reaches the ball. He reacts by angrily flinging it over the boundary rope. What now?

30

At 11:30am sharp in a village match, both teams file out, thinking they are fielding. It turns out there's been a dispute, which you missed, over who won the toss and what was decided. What action do you take?

The batting side need one run to win, and the striker needs four runs for his hundred. The bowler delivers a no ball, which the striker hits for six. Does the striker get his hundred, and what do the scorers record?

32

TREVILLION

31

As a batsman dives for the crease, his bat accidentally slips from his grasp, flies forwards and knocks all three stumps out of the ground just as the wicketkeeper was about to break the wicket. What is your decision?

33

In a County Championship match, the striker receives a high bouncer that loops way over his head. He tries to hook it, but only manages to top-edge the ball to fine leg, who catches it. Out or not out?

With two wickets remaining, the batting side need four off the last two balls to win. The striker top-edges the ball high into the air and sets off for a run. This will bring the other batsman, a prolific scorer, to the striker's end. However, the wicketkeeper lets the ball drop, where it strikes middle stump. The fielders say the striker was bowled out and the No. 11 should face the final delivery. What now?

34

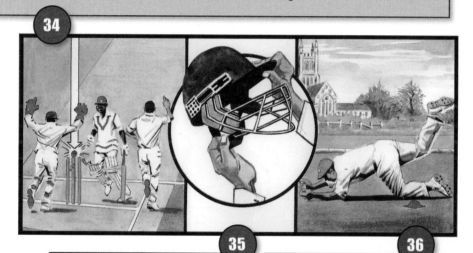

35

A batsman who has scored over 100 is found at the interval to have been receiving coaching through a receiver in his helmet. What action do you take?

36

A fielder in the outfield dives to stop a powerful drive. As he grabs the ball, his red handkerchief falls to the grass – confusing both batsmen, who mistake it for the ball. As they run again, the fielder returns the ball, and the bails are whipped off. Both batsmen complain. Out or not?

Two exceptionally fast bowlers have opened the innings and are firing down many lifting deliveries. The batsmen complain that the wicketkeeper at the end of each over – in a voice loud enough for them to hear – shouts to the bowlers that the batsmen are scared witless and he can see their legs shaking. They say that this is affecting their concentration. What do you do?

38

37

A sharp, rising delivery raps the striker on the glove and loops towards his wicket. He quickly whips one hand off the bat and knocks the ball away with that hand. There is an appeal. What is your decision?

39

With four minutes of playing time left, the last pair at the wicket are fighting to avoid defeat. The striker is clean bowled by an unplayable yorker that sends his middle stump cartwheeling. But both batsmen remain at the crease. The fielding side are excitedly celebrating but no one appeals. What next?

Just before tea, with only a handful of runs needed for a result and a hint of rain in the air, the two batsmen ask to delay the interval and complete the match. Do you allow this?

40

41

42

Before lunch, the slips have spilled four easy catches, so their captain orders them to stay on the field for 20 minutes during the break to practise. But the opposing team say that would give them an unfair advantage. Do you let them?

A fielder keeps bowling the ball back to the wicketkeeper, bouncing it on a hard, bare patch on the outfield as he does so. The batsmen complain that he's deliberately changing the condition of the ball. What do you do?

43

A batsman blocks a ball, which spins behind him and stops dead. As he turns, he accidentally kicks it into the stumps. The bails fall and the bowler appeals. What now?

45

A batsman mistimes a sweep shot and falls to his knees. As he does so, the ball hits him and rolls towards the stumps, but he stops it, using the same hand that is holding the bat. The opposition appeal. What now?

44

A village side whose equipment has been vandalised have improvised a solution by setting up three branches as stumps in regulation size. Do you play the game?

A medium-pace bowler suddenly stops in the middle of his run up. It seems as if he has misjudged his run, but he immediately carries on and clean bowls the batsman. The batsman is furious. What is your decision?

46

47

A fielder realises he has no time to pick up the ball if he is to run out the batsman, so he kicks the ball at the wicket instead. It misses, but hits the bat, rebounds onto the wicket and displaces the bails before the batsman is able to make his ground. Out or not out?

48

With light rain getting heavier, the batting side, who have all their wickets standing, are running sharp singles, needing just 20 runs to win. But at every delivery, the wicketkeeper whips off the bails, then waits for you to replace them. The batsman insists this is deliberate time wasting. What now?

A batsman hammers an overpitched ball delivered by a fast bowler. The close-to-the-bat fielder ducks as the ball hits his helmet and flies straight back at the face of the batsman, who instinctively swipes the ball away with his bat. The fielding side appeal on the grounds that the batsman hit the ball twice. What is your decision?

50

49

In fading light, a fast bowler who takes an unusually long run up to the wicket keeps stopping and starting his run up. The batting captain suggests you tell the fielding captain to take the bowler off, arguing that in fading light the fast bowler represents a danger to the batsman. What is your decision?

51

A batsman advances well out of his crease and attempts to slog the slow bowler's full toss. He misses and the ball makes contact with his chest. But before the ball has fallen to the ground, he sweeps it to the boundary rope. Do the runs count?

A batsman manages to get his bat down on a yorker, only to see it roll back onto his middle stump. Both bails are disturbed with the two ends of each bail resting on the middle stump out of their grooves. The bowler having continued to run, now stands over the stumps waiting for the bails to drop. When they fail to do so he appeals on the grounds the bails are not in their start-of-play position and the wicket is in effect broken. Is he right?

52

53

A batsman attempts to hit a ball that you have signalled a wide. He wildly overreaches and falls well out of his crease. A fielder collects the ball, throws it to the wicketkeeper, who stumps the batsman. Out or not out?

54

As the umpire, you recognise that the batsman is clearly LBW, but there is no appeal, so you call over. The bowler starts his walk back, ready to bowl the next over. Suddenly the captain of the fielding side, who has had second thoughts on the LBW incident, calls to the bowler to stop and appeals. What is your decision?

A fielder who is positioned very close to the wicket and has been hit a few times, has taken the precaution of wearing a protective rubber waistcoat under his shirt and shin pads under his trousers. The ball is hit towards him, strikes the protective waistcoat, bounces in the air, and is caught by a slip fielder. The batsman claims the ball, having hit a fielder, would normally drop to the ground. What do you do?

55

56

In a village match, a batsman hits a high ball, which evades all the fielders, just as a dog runs onto the field inside the boundary ropes and catches the ball in its mouth. A fielder calls the dog over, takes the ball from its mouth and appeals for a catch. What is your decision?

57

As a bowler runs up to deliver, he notices that the non-striker has left his ground. He stops and tells the batsman that he will run him out the next time he transgresses. Two balls later the non-striker leaves his ground early, the bowler breaks the wicket lawfully and appeals. Out or not out?

An ambidextrous slow bowler decides to mix up his deliveries during an over, switching from bowling left-handed to right-handed during his run up. The batsman does not object. Do you intervene?

58

59

Between overs you notice a fielder taking a spare ball out of his pocket and practising catches. The opposition captain complains. What now?

60

A batsman walks out for a village match just hours after getting married in his whites. The first delivery he faces is a screamer. It bounces high and clips his buttonhole flower, knocking it onto the wicket. Both bails are dislodged. Out or not out?

With only two wickets standing, a star opener and tailender are chasing 15 runs to win. As they cross in the middle on the way to a quick single, the tailender spots the ball flying towards the end to which the star man is running. So he makes a quick call. The two batsmen stop and double back to avoid the opener being run out. What is your ruling?

61

62

63

A fast delivery knocks the bails to the ground. The bowler appeals and you give the batsman out, but he refuses to walk. He says the keeper broke the wicket. But before you can give your verdict, the bowler withdraws his appeal. He says he'll get the batsman out next ball anyway. What now?

In running up to deliver, a bowler spots that the striker is standing out of his ground. Quick as a flash, he throws the ball with all his might, catches the striker by surprise, and the ball breaks his wicket. There is an appeal. What is your verdict?

On a turning wicket, a slow bowler is spinning the ball with exaggerated movement both sides of the wicket. The wicketkeeper, close to the stumps with the sun shining on his back, is annoying the batsman. His shadow, which falls directly over the wicket, is continuously moving from side to side, echoing his movements. Finally, the two batsmen ask you to request the wicketkeeper to limit his distracting exaggerated movements behind the wicket. Will you do this?

65

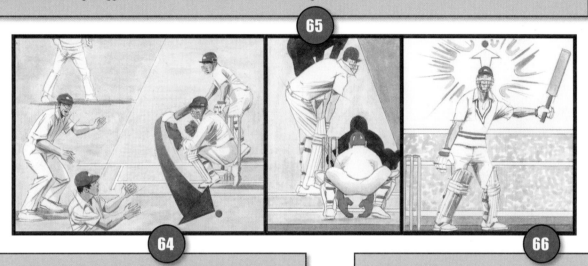

64

A wicketkeeper is injured and leaves the field. He is replaced by the 12th man and his captain dons the gloves. The captain has a nightmare behind the wicket, conceding numerous byes and dropping catches. He wants to give the gloves to one of his specialist close catchers. Can you allow this second change?

66

A batsman attempts to duck a bouncer, but it hits his helmet, flies straight up into the air, and as the ball drops, the batsman – unmoved and unharmed by the blow on his helmet – belts the ball over the boundary rope. Do you award a six?

In a county match, a slow bowler has been hit consecutively for six by the batsman advancing well down the wicket and turning the delivery into a full toss. The bowler decides to pitch the next ball well short, but this time the batsman has not advanced down the wicket, he allows the ball to bounce twice, then hammers it over the boundary rope. What now?

68

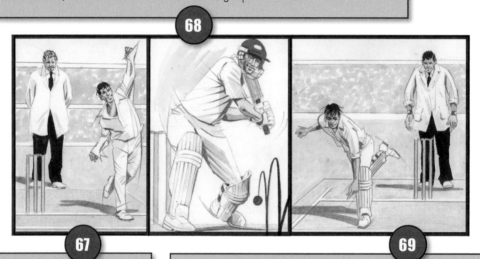

67

A slow bowler is wearing a shirt at least two sizes too large. The unbuttoned sleeve covers his bowling hand until he releases the ball and the batsman demands he buttons up his sleeve. What is your decision?

69

A bowler has delivered four successive no balls by overstepping the popping crease, from which the batsman has failed to score. He fails to hit the next no ball, which strikes him on the pads and lands at his feet. The frustrated batsman picks up the ball, stands well inside the crease, and bowls a perfectly good ball back to the bowler. The bowler appeals. What do you do?

A batsman plays a shot down the wicket. Both batsmen set off for a run, while the bowler races to collect the ball for a possible run out. The ball stops midway between the bowler and the batsman running towards him. If the batsman changes course to avoid a collision, he increases the possibility of a run out, so he continues. The inevitable collision sends the bowler sprawling and the batsmen complete the run. The fielding side claim obstruction. The batsman insists it was his 'right of way'. What is your decision?

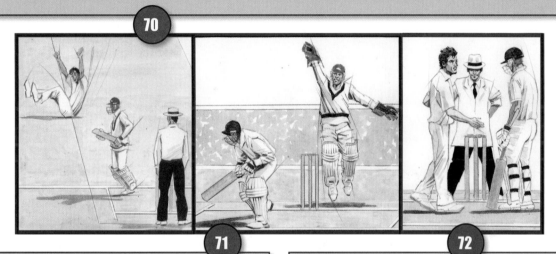

70

71

72

In a village match, the wicketkeeper appeals for a catch behind the wicket. You signal the batsman out but the batsman tells the wicketkeeper his bat did not touch the ball. Shame-faced, the wicketkeeper agrees. Can the batsman who has been given out, resume his innings?

On a hot day the captain of the fielding team requests an extra drink interval at the completion of the over. A batsman overhears his request and walks up shaking his head, stressing it is not necessary, adding that he acts as the captain when the team captain is not on the field of play. What do you do?

A batsman gives a faint edge to the last ball before lunch, which is caught by the wicketkeeper. Nobody appeals but the batsman walks immediately. When the fielders realise the batsman's act of sportsmanship, they applaud but still do not appeal, and both batsmen and the fielders disappear into the pavilion. The captain of the batting side, not pleased with his team-mate's sporting behaviour, insists he returns to the crease after lunch, claiming that a batsman can only be out on appeal. Is he right?

73

74

75

In a county match, an injured batsman who has a runner hammers the ball through the air directly at the runner, who ducks as the ball hits him and rebounds straight to a fielder who catches the ball and appeals. Is the batsman out?

A batsman, who has been hit a number of times on his gloves by a fiery fast bowler, is bravely batting on, in spite of pain in both hands. When the next ball from the bowler rears up, he takes both hands off the bat. The ball strikes the bat as it falls to the ground and is caught. The fielder appeals. What is your decision?

On a windy day a large piece of sticky paper, probably from a spectator's packed lunch, blows onto the field. The ball from a lofted drive lands on the sticky paper and becomes wrapped up in it. At no time did the ball touch the grass. A fielder picks up the ball still covered in the sticky paper and struggles to unwrap it while the batsmen cross for another run. The fielder then appeals for a catch with pieces of the sticky paper still on the ball. What is your decision?

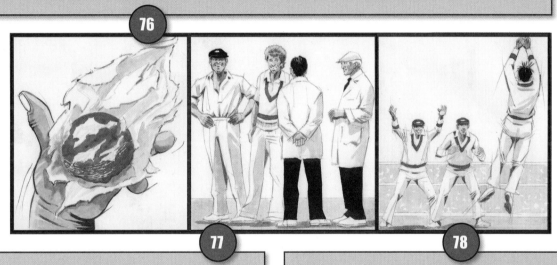

76

77

78

In a village match, the two captains, who are old friends, ask if they can play 12-a-side because both 12th men are very handy batsmen and it's not in the spirit of village cricket if they don't get an innings. You agree. They also ask that 12 players be allowed to field. Do you permit this?

A fielder in a village match attempts to catch a high ball and falls awkwardly. Shaken up, he leaves the field and the 12th man takes his place. Later you notice that the original fielder has returned and, having taken a high catch, is appealing. The 12th man is still on the field of play. What action do you take?

The wicketkeeper is standing up to the stumps, when the usually medium-pace bowler sends down an extra-fast one that passes the bat, strikes the keeper on the arm, and rebounds onto the wicket, removing the bails. The batsman is still in his crease, but is he out?

81

79

In a village match, a batsman drives the ball straight down the pitch where, without bouncing, it somehow lodges between the stumps. The bowler pulls it out and appeals for a catch. What now?

80

The incoming batsman is stepping onto the field, when a team-mate dashes past him, telling him to go back. His captain has changed the batting order. The fielding captain protests. What do you do?

A striker facing a slow bowler plays a smart defensive shot that drops the ball at his feet as he sets off for a run. His partner, who is well advanced down the pitch, calls out that the ball has spun back towards his wicket. A close-in fielder sees the opportunity for a run out and races in, but just as he attempts to pick up the ball, the batsman knocks it away to avoid the possibility of being bowled. What is your decision?

83

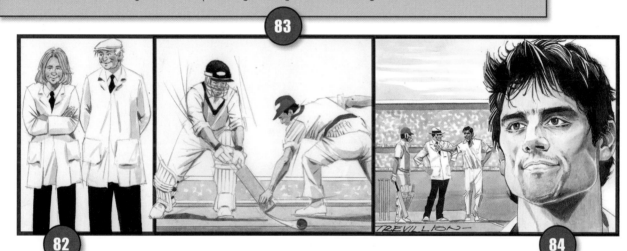

82

The visiting team in a village match are greeted by the two umpires – a married couple. They inform both captains that the husband will stand at the bowler's end and his wife will stand at the striker's end on the off-side instead of the traditional on-side. Both captains are unsure if this is in the laws of the MCC, but are happy to go ahead with the match. Have the two captains made the right decision?

84

A non-striker stands on the same side of the wicket from which the ball is being delivered. The bowler, whose action takes him close to the wicket, complains. What action do you take?

On a turning pitch, the batsman comes down the wicket to the slow bowler, confident that, because he advances more than a third of the way down the pitch, he is too far away from the wicket for the umpire to justify LBW. Is he right?

85

86

87

A captain, who has just won the toss, informs his opposite number that he must confer with his team and coach before deciding whether to bat or field. Do you allow this?

A right-handed batsman maintains his batting stance (left foot leading), but plays a cross bat left-handed shot (left arm leading) that clears the boundary. The fielding side claim that the switch-handed stroke is now illegal. Are they right or do you signal a six?

A batsman, needing one run off the last ball to win, goes for a quick single, but accidentally collides with the bowler. While the non-striker makes his ground, the striker is hurt and cannot complete his run. But when the ball reaches the fielding captain near the stumps, he says it would not be fair to go for a run out, and you should award the win to the batting side instead. What do you do?

89

88

A bowler fails to take a catch, unintentionally deflecting the ball on to the stumps. It knocks the bails off while the non-striker is out of his ground – and then without hitting the ground, rebounds off the stumps back to the bowler who this time catches it cleanly. Who is out?

90

A batsman walks an easy single as the ball is returned to the bowler. But the bowler notices that the batsman is now sitting on the handle of his bat. His feet are outside the popping crease, but the bat is grounded a few inches behind it. The bowler removes the bails and appeals. What do you do?

91 You have miscounted the number of balls in an over and the seventh ball yields a wicket. The non-striker highlights the counting error before the batsman has left the field. What is your decision?

92 A fielder attempts a catch. He makes contact, but fails to hold on and crashes to the ground. As he falls, his shirt comes out of his trousers and the ball lands on his shirt tail. He picks it up and appeals. Out or not out?

93 A slow bowler has a wrist action that conceals the ball with the back of the hand, and the hand turns suddenly before releasing a quick delivery. He is wearing a red sweatband on his wrist and both batsmen complain that this makes it difficult to judge the ball's flight. They call for the sweatband to be replaced by a white one. What do you do?

A batsman has second thoughts about running after playing a defensive shot, so he turns and dives back to reach his crease. But in doing so, his bat hits the ball on the ground, knocking it away from the stumps and from the fielders. They appeal. What now?

94

TREVILLION

95

The home team need three runs to win. The No. 10 and No. 11 batsmen are at the wicket. The No. 10 hits the last ball of the over and runs a very quick single, right down the middle of the pitch. You warn him, but on the next ball he does it again. What do you do?

96

A village batsman needs four runs to complete his maiden century. He takes an almighty swing at the ball, aiming to hit a six, but he succeeds only in edging the ball straight down. Instead of the ball hitting his wicket, it hits his raised boot, which sends it soaring off over the boundary rope. What do you award?

The batting team need five runs from three balls to win. After the bowler delivers, he slips and falls heavily. The ball is hit for four to level the scores, but the bowler gets up holding his shoulder and says he cannot bowl the last two balls of the match. What now?

97

A fielder leaps high in the air and gets his hand to the ball, but fumbles it. The ball drops straight down and lodges inside his shirt. The fielder takes the ball out of his shirt and claims the catch. Is the batsman out?

99

98

The away team are put into bat. After two hours, a visiting player is seen driving into the ground and padding up. At the fall of the fourth wicket he strides out, but the home captain, knowing he is the opposition's top scorer, claims that the incoming batsman, having arrived late, cannot bat higher than No. 7. What is your ruling?

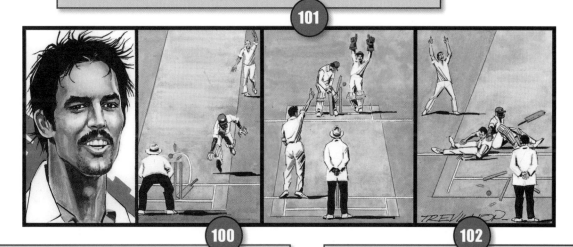

101

A slow spin bowler, who has been taking four strides back before turning to run up and deliver the ball, decides halfway through an over to take only two strides back before turning and delivering, and takes out the middle stump. The batsman protests that he was not ready. Out or not out?

100

A batsman turns for a sharp second run and accidentally drops his bat. A fielder tries to run him out only to see his on-target throw hit the bat and bounce wide of the wicket. But the impact also knocks the bat into the stumps, which dislodges the bails. There's an appeal. What is your decision?

102

A batsman sets off for a quick single, but collides with the bowler, and both fall to the ground. The bowler's arm lands within the crease, and the batsman has his hand on the bowler's shoulder. A fielder throws down the stumps and appeals. Is the batsman in his ground?

A high shot looks like it's heading for six until a fielder on the boundary steps back over the ropes, leaps upwards and knocks the ball forwards over the field of play, then enters the field and makes a clean catch. The fielders appeal but the striker stands his ground. What now?

103

104

A batsman is clean bowled, but the non-striker says it was a no ball. He points out that part of the bowler's front foot landed past the middle stump. What is your decision?

105

At a village match, the visiting team are one man short and asks if it can deploy one of the player's girlfriends. But the opposition know that she plays at a high level in the women's game, so protest on the basis that she's not male. Do you allow her to play?

107 A fielder jumps to take a high catch and gets his fingers to the ball, but he cannot hold it. He drops the ball onto the sunglasses resting on his cap, it ricochets off, and a colleague takes the catch. Out or not out?

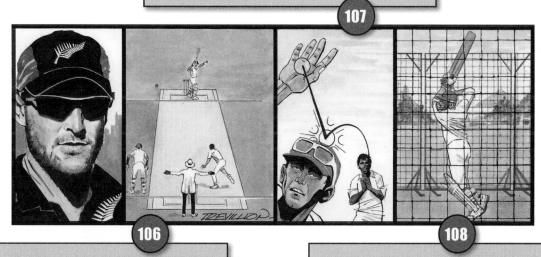

106 A batting team with wickets in hand are chasing quick runs to win a One-Day International with the light fading fast. The bowlers appear to deliberately bowl two or three wides an over to avoid defeat. What do you do?

108 When three quick wickets fall, a lower-order batsman dashes straight to the crease from the nets where he was warming up. The visiting captain protests, saying the workout just before taking his place was unlawful. Do you agree?

On an overcast day during which the sun frequently bursts through the clouds, a batsman is at the crease with his favourite bat polished to a shine. The fielding side accuse him of dazzling them when the sun reflects off his shiny bat. A fielder who has already complained about the glare then misses an easy catch and claims he was blinded by the bat. There's uproar. What do you do?

A bowler tries for a run out. With one bail already down following a previous run-out attempt, he dislodges the other and appeals. But the batsmen insist it's not out. They say he should have removed a stump. Are they right?

Before the start of play, the away captain tells you he wants to enforce the follow-on, but unbeknown to you and your fellow umpire, he has failed to tell the opposing captain. The home side are furious, saying that the away captain must now wait until lunch before enforcing the follow-on. Are they right?

The batsmen sprint for a sharp single and crash into each other mid-wicket. The wicketkeeper whips off the bails, then throws the ball down to the bowler, who knocks over the wicket at his end. Both batsmen are in the centre of the pitch and both wickets are down. Which one is out?

112

113

An unusually short batsman in a 20-over match damages the straps on one of his black pads. The only available spare that will fit him is white. Can he play on with one white pad and one black pad?

114

An eager batsman advances for a slow delivery and misses the ball. The wicketkeeper quickly moves in for a stumping, but his cap falls off and dislodges a bail a split second before the ball hits the wicket. Out or not out?

In the last over of a Twenty20 innings, the striking batsman digs out a yorker and is called through for a single by the non-striker. The ball then spins towards the wicket, but is prevented from hitting the stumps by the non-striker as he makes his ground. The fielding side appeal. What is your decision?

115

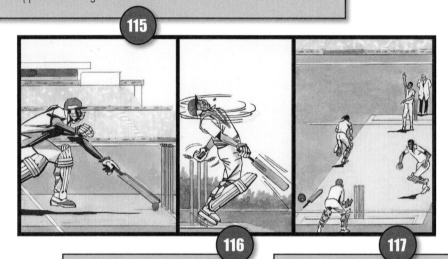

116

A batsman is troubled by a wasp just as a slow bowler releases a delivery. As he recoils, he swipes off his bails by mistake. There's an appeal. What now?

117

The batting side need two runs off the last ball to win. The striker hits the delivery towards the long boundary and, to help them run faster, both batsmen drop their bats and shed their helmets before starting their run. Do you intervene?

118 A batsman drops his bat when racing off for two runs. Struggling to make his ground for the second, he dives forwards and gets two fingers on his bat handle. The bat is grounded outside and inside the crease before the bails fall. What is your decision?

119 During a drinks break in a village match, you spot the bowler dropping the match ball into his glass of orange juice. The batting side complain he has deliberately changed the ball's dynamics, but the bowler insists it was an accident. What now?

120 A batsman skies a shot. As he hesitates, the non-striker shouts, 'My call, stop there'. But the fielder nearest the ball hears it too and pulls out of the catch, thinking the shout came from a fellow fielder. What do you do?

Following an unsuccessful run out in which the wicket was broken, the ball rebounded into the outfield and the batsmen set off for a second run. The fielder close to the wicket asks you to help him quickly rebuild the wicket as the fielder who is about to pick up the ball has an excellent opportunity to hit the stumps directly and run out one of the batsmen. How do you respond?

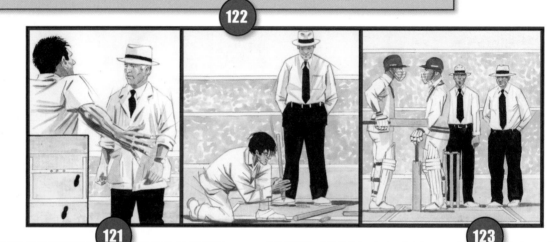

Before starting his next spell of bowling, a fast bowler, who has been no-balled three times before being taken off, asks you if he can have a practice run up and if you will check the placement of his lead foot. Do you agree to this?

In a championship decider with the home side fielding, the crowd sense victory as the wickets tumble. The spectators cheer wildly with every delivery stride, distracting the two batsmen at the crease. They turn to you and your fellow umpire and request you intervene. What is your decision?

After a short break, a pace bowler prepares for his second spell. You assume his action will be unchanged, so you don't check with him, and you don't tell the batsman what to expect. On the first delivery the batsman shoulders arms and is clean bowled. What happens now?

A close fielder's cap flies off as he fumbles a catch and the ball lands inside it. The batsman reacts by picking up the cap and allowing the ball to drop on to the grass. Is he out for obstructing the field?

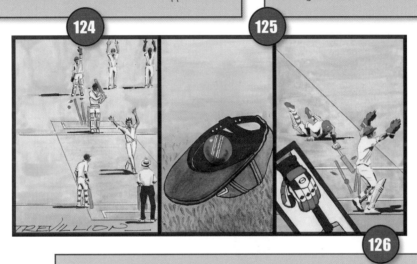

A batsman hammers a straight drive that hits his colleague's bat and knocks it out of his hand. In playing the shot, the striker drops his own bat. The batsmen run, and the non-striker dives for his ground, but falls short as the wicket is put down. But his hand is touching the handle of the striker's bat, part of which is grounded behind the popping crease. The fielding side appeal. Out or not out?

Off the first ball of the over, the batsman snicks the ball and turns to witness the wicketkeeper take a spectacular one-handed catch and appeal. You give the batsman out, but the batsman stands his ground. He questions the elaborate, large half-moon shaped webbing between the finger and thumb, which he believes is not allowed within the laws and which definitely enabled the wicketkeeper to make the catch. What is your decision?

127

128

129

During the morning play, the three slip fielders have dropped four straightforward catches. The fielding captain asks you if, during the lunch break, the slip fielders can come out ten minutes early and practise taking catches, standing in their slip-fielding positions behind the wicket. Do you allow this?

A bowler repeatedly switches side, bowling over and around the wicket. The batsman has become agitated with the constant change of sides and the non-striker flatly refuses to change sides. The bowler complains to you. What do you do?

After struggling badly in a limited-overs game, a batsman is caught. But the fielding captain tells you he wants to withdraw the appeal and let the batsman continue. What do you do?

130

A ball beats the bat and hits the wicket, but does not disturb the stumps. However, one bail flies into the air, where it is caught flamboyantly by the wicketkeeper who appeals. Our or not out?

131

132

A No. 11 batsman, who has had a season full of ducks, walks out wearing a Donald Duck mask – a gift from his team-mates – to start his innings on the final day. Do you intervene?

A batsman playing a defensive stroke hits the ball, which spins back towards his stumps. The batsman places his bat on top of the bails to prevent them from being dislodged. In the event, the ball stops short of the stumps, but the bowler appeals. What is your call?

134

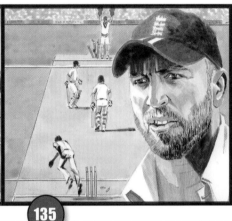

133

To avoid being hit by a beamer, a batsman lurches forwards and steps out of his ground. The wicketkeeper catches the ball, whips off the bails and appeals for a run out. What now?

135

Both batsmen – a top-order and a tail-ender – are stranded in the middle of the pitch. The bails are whipped off at the bowler's end, but before an appeal is made, which would have run out the tail-ender, the quick-thinking bowler throws down the wicket at the other end and appeals in order to run out the top-order batsman. What is your decision?

During a period of hostile but fair fast bowling, the batsman has successfully played the short, sharp rising ball down in front of his feet. When he sees another ball pitched short, the close-in fielder moves swiftly and then dives forward to make the catch and appeal. The batsman is not pleased, pointing out that the sudden swift movement of the fielder just before he had made contact with the ball was unfair, unsporting and not within the laws of cricket. Do you agree?

136

137

In a village match, you are the only umpire available. The two captains ask you if the local vicar, a keen cricket follower who always comes to watch their games, can officiate (he has previously agreed he would be very happy to do so). What is your decision?

138

A batsman ducks out of the way of a vicious bouncer. The ball strikes his protective arm shield, deflects over the heads of the slips, and flies over the boundary rope. Is it a six?

In an unsuccessful run out, just one bail is removed. The ball travels into the outfield while the batsmen set off for another run. An exceptionally fast fielder quickly returns the ball to the wicketkeeper, who removes the other bail with the batsman out of his ground and appeals. The run-out batsman, back in the crease, informs the wicketkeeper that at least one stump needs to be pulled out of the ground to complete a run out after the wicket is broken. Is he right?

139

140

141

A batsman's drive splays the stumps at the other end and he starts to run. A fielder quickly hurls the ball at the broken wicket, which it strikes before the batsman makes his ground. However, because the wicket has already been destroyed, the bails cannot be removed. Can you award a run out?

Prior to a village match, in an effort to increase the size of the playing area, the home team had a huge tree in the outfield chopped down. But the stump remains slightly above ground level. Both teams are happy with the larger outfield and are still keen to play the match. What is your decision?

A delivery comes off the striker's foot without a shot being offered, and races away. As the batsmen take one leg bye and try for a second, a fielder goes for a run out. But the ball misses and shoots off over the boundary. How many leg byes do you give?

142

A batsman strikes the ball straight back towards the non-striker. Instinctively, the non-striker puts out his gloved hand and catches the ball. The fielding side appeal. Out or not out?

144

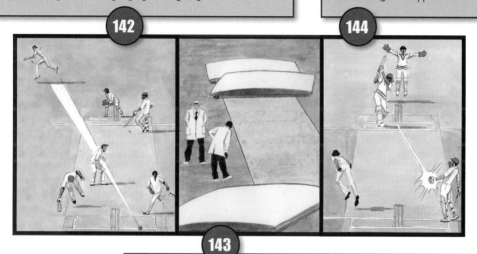

143

Following a rain delay, you and your fellow umpire decide that the ground is fit for play. The away captain is delighted with your decision, but the home captain, whose side are fielding, believes the conditions are still too dangerous and there is a risk of injury to his players. He insists it is necessary to allow more time before play can restart. What is your decision?

In a village match, the striking batsman is wearing a large, floppy jumper and holds his bat at shoulder height before the bowler delivers the ball. His batting partner is not wearing a jumper and adopts an orthodox batting stance. As the bowler starts his long walk back, the striking batsman swiftly removes his jumper, drops it behind the stumps, and adopts an orthodox batting stance. The bowler, distracted by the batsman's tactics, bowls a long hop, which is hammered for a six. What is your decision?

147

145

A batsman just manages to get the top half of his bat to a short, fast, rising ball, which loops off the bat and, still in the air, threatens to hit the wicket. The batsman then hits the ball again, which flies straight to a fielder who takes the catch and appeals. Out or not out?

146

Attempting a catch, the wicketkeeper falls awkwardly, is injured, and has to leave the field. The fielding captain asks if the substitute fielder can keep wicket. The batting team's captain, who is one of the batsmen, has no objection to the request. What is your decision?

A fast bowler appears to have tripped himself up when delivering an extra-fast ball, but somehow he recovers his balance and sends down a ball that knocks out the middle stump. The batsman complains his concentration was broken when he believed the bowler was about to fall and hurt himself. What is your decision?

148

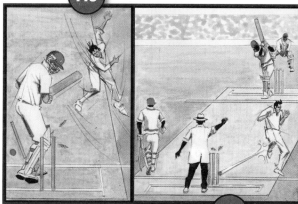

149

When a batsman hammers a no ball straight back down the wicket, the bowler takes evasive action. But the ball hits him and rebounds into the wicket, removing the bails with the non-striker out of the crease. The bowler appeals. Out or not out?

150

An opening batsman, who has been out 'for a duck' on his last four visits to the crease, does not appreciate seeing the opening fast bowler wearing a large sweatband on which is written 'DUCK' in large letters. He asks you to tell him to remove the insulting item. What do you do?

The opening batsman is out 'for a golden duck'. But three balls later, you realise there is an extra fielder playing. Do you reinstate the batsman and re-bowl the over; play on, after removing the fielder; or decide something else?

152

151

A batsman on 99 runs is disgusted with himself after giving the bowler an easy chance at a catch. With the ball in midair, he hurls his bat away in anger. It distracts the bowler, who misses the catch. What do you do?

153

A spin bowler loops up a very high, very slow delivery. The batsman advances out of his crease and you give him LBW when the ball hits his pad. But the square-leg umpire intervenes, saying the delivery was so slow it would never have reached the stumps. What now?

Four fielders in the slips have fixed together two wristbands with a rubber band. They repeatedly throw this to one another during a fast bowler's exceptionally long walk back before he starts his run up to the wicket. Both batsmen complain that this is illegal catching practice during play. What is your ruling?

154

155

A slow bowler, who takes just one stride before delivering the ball, races through an over. Both batsmen complain they do not have enough time to get set before the next ball comes down. What action do you take?

156

When an extremely athletic fielder takes a catch, he performs a triple somersault, leaps high in the air, completes a twirl, lands and bows to the wildly cheering crowd. The two batsmen are not happy. They believe this is not in the spirit of the game. Do you agree?

A snick off the first ball of the opening over results in a catch behind the wicket. You signal out. The opening batsman shows you his brand new bat and insists he did not get a touch. Any ball movement during his stroke was down to the bowler. He goes on to ask, 'If I did snick the ball, identify the new ball's red cherry mark on the edge of the bat.' How do you respond?

157

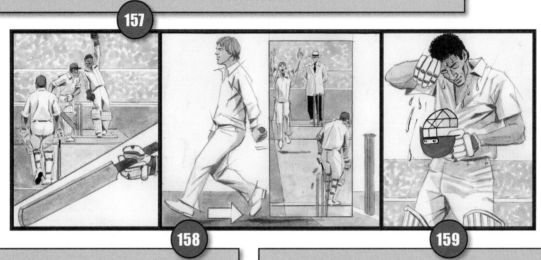

158

In a village match, the crowd cheer wildly when a young slow bowler comes on. They cheer even louder when he starts his run up with his back to the wicket. Just before his delivery stride, he turns, bowls and knocks the bewildered batsman's middle stump out. Out or not out?

159

On an extremely hot and humid day when the batsman appears to be experiencing discomfort with his helmet, he is clean bowled, without offering a stroke. The batsman takes off his helmet. His face is dripping with sweat, which he attempts to wipe from his eyes, and which has temporarily blinded him. What do you do?

In a village match, an elderly, overweight batsman who has obviously had a rich meal the night before, repeatedly passes wind at the wicket. The wicketkeeper complains that the foul smell means he is forced to turn his head away and risk missing a catch or stumping behind the wicket. You suggest he stands well back, but the wicketkeeper complains this puts him at a disadvantage. How do you respond?

160

The close-in fielder attempts a run out by kicking the ball at the wicket, but as he does so, his boot flies off. The ball soars up and lands in the boot, which flattens the stumps. The fielder appeals with the batsman well short of the crease. Out or not out?

161

An exceptional spinner of the ball, who bowls with his cap on, delivers a ball that turns viciously, beats the batsman's forward defensive stroke, and removes the off stump. The bowler appeals. The batsman points to the bowler's cap, which has fallen off and is now on the ground. He insists it distracted him. What do you do?

A slow bowler walks up while tossing a ball from one hand to the other. Then he releases a perfectly legal delivery with considerable spin that removes the batsman's off stump. The batsman complains that the ball tossing was a distraction. What is your decision?

163

164

165

A fast bowler sends down a yorker. The batsman stabs down hard. He misses the ball, but the ball also misses the wicket. Unfortunately, when the batsman stabbed down, a small piece of the base of his bat broke away and flew on to hit the stumps, and a bail was removed. Out or not out?

A batsman just manages to get his bat on a wickedly spinning ball only to see it spin away towards the wicket. The batsman, reacting instinctively, kicks the ball away and it rolls over the boundary rope. Do the four runs count?

During a match, a batsman notices that his favourite bat from the 1990s needs urgent repairs. He secures the damage with elaborate bandaging. The fielding captain claims that the bat is now more than the maximum width allowed. What now?

166

Having won the toss on the last four meetings and put opposition in to bat, and then lost the match, the visiting captain asks you to permit the home captain simply to choose to bat or bowl without a toss. What is your decision?

168

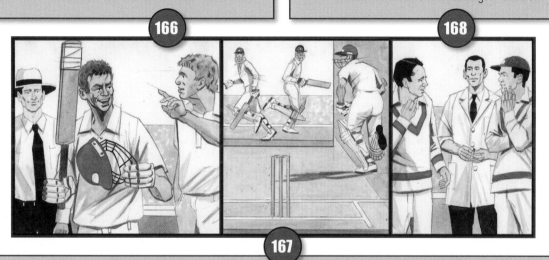

167

A batsman hammers the ball, which pierces the field and looks a certain four. The batsmen therefore stop running after almost completing the first run. But a fielder stops the ball just short of the boundary and returns it to the wicketkeeper. The batsmen have already returned to their creases. You signal a short run and five penalty runs. Should the five runs immediately be taken off the scoreboard? Or should the five penalty runs appear on the scoreboard when the fielding team start their second innings? Alternatively, should the five penalty runs be added to the fielding team's first innings total?

In an attempted run out, a fielder throws the ball, removing both bails. But the batsman has already made his ground. The ball runs loose and the batsmen go for a second run. This time the batsman is well out of his ground when another fielder hits the same wicket, but all three stumps stay in the ground. Is the batsman out?

169

TREVILLION

170

A batsman recoils from an exceptionally high bouncer. As you signal wide, the batsman stumbles back and breaks his wicket. The bowler appeals. Out or not out?

171

During a fast delivery, the ball slips out of the bowler's hand. It lands just short of the batsman and stops dead. But the striker takes a swipe at it anyway and is caught. The bowler appeals. What do you do?

It is the last ball of a one-day match and the scores are tied. The injured striker has a runner. The striker manages to fend the final delivery away and both he and his runner set off for a quick single, but after a few steps the striker pulls up in pain. The runner makes his ground just before the ball is thrown in and breaks the wicket at the bowler's end. There is an appeal. Out or not out?

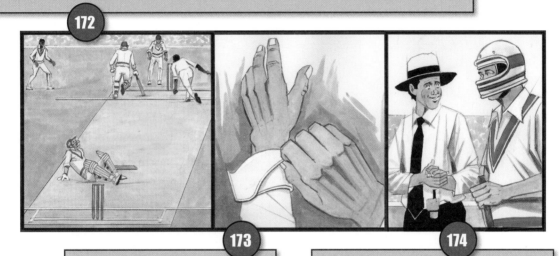

172

173

A bowler has turned back the cuffs of his shirt sleeves. They are now twice their normal thickness. The bowler then shines the ball on the double thickness cuffs. Do you intervene?

174

In a county match, a batsman arrives at the crease wearing a motorcycle helmet, explaining that after two overs the standard cricket helmet gives him a violent headache. Do you permit this?

A spin bowler attempts to surprise the batsman and decides to bowl an extra-fast delivery. But he loses his grip on the ball and it sails high in the air. The batsman, who has advanced down the wicket, looks back to see the ball fall and remove both bails. The bowler appeals, but the batsman claims he believed he heard you call dead ball the moment the ball slipped from the bowler's grip. What do you do?

176

175

A right-handed slow bowler is becoming frustrated by a batsman who, between deliveries, repeatedly changes his stance. The bowler, being ambidextrous, decides to switch the ball to his left hand. He succeeds in bowling the batsman and appeals. Out or not out?

177

In a village match on an extremely hot and humid day, the home captain asks if his team can field wearing shorts. What is your decision?

Attempting to hit the ball twice in defence of his wicket, a batsman stops as a close-in fielder dives for a catch, gets his hand to the ball, but fails to complete the catch. The batsman then knocks the ball away with his bat and the fielder appeals. What is your decision?

179

178

In a county match, a rare species of butterfly settles on top of the bails. Various attempts to get the butterfly to fly away fail. How long would you allow before you take further measures?

180

In fading light, the batting team are hanging on for a draw. The two bowlers complain that the batsmen are wasting time by repeatedly stopping them at the start of their run up, signalling they are not ready to take strike. What do you do?

181 The wicketkeeper drops a straightforward catch, but seeing the batsman is out of his crease, kicks the ball onto the stumps, removes the bails and appeals. Out or not out?

182 Although you have signalled a no ball, the wicketkeeper has spotted the batsman is out of his crease. He removes the bails and appeals, but the batsman had not tried to run. What do you do?

183 A batsman knocks the ball towards a fielder and sets off for a run. He stops when the fielder throws the ball to the wicketkeeper. To avoid being hit by the off-line throw, the batsman steps out of his crease. The wicketkeeper collects the ball, removes the bails and appeals. What is your decision?

Before the bowler runs up, the batsman notices there are three fielders behind square leg. Knowing that it should be a no ball, he takes a wild swipe and is bowled. But your colleague did not see the third fielder, so didn't call a no ball. The batsman stands his ground in protest. What do you do?

185

184

186

A batsman plays the ball and sets off for a quick single. But his batting partner, seeing a fielder racing in to get the ball, immediately shouts 'No!'. As the batsman stops, he loses his footing and slips backwards into the stumps. Is he out?

A batsman hits the ball almost vertically in the air and goes for a quick single. But the non-striker, seeing the ball will land on the stumps, sprints and dives forward, flattening them before the ball drops. The fielders appeal. What is your decision?

187 After a heated exchange, the two captains approach you and ask, 'When can a non-striker lawfully leave his ground?' What is your response?

189 A fielder dives full length, crashes into the boundary boards, and gets his hand to the ball, stopping the four runs. But the knocked-back ball hits one of the displaced boards, which is now well inside the field of play. What is your decision?

188 A batsman blasts the ball straight at the bowler, who goes to catch it in one hand. But simultaneously the bowler notices the non-striking batsman, a star player, is out of his crease, so he diverts the ball onto the stumps instead, and appeals for a run out. What is your decision?

191 A fast bowler is far from happy. He has been no balled on three occasions. To express his disapproval of your decisions, with his next delivery he deliberately oversteps with his front foot by at least 12 inches. What action do you take?

190 In a county match, the home captain asks if at the drink intervals each of his team can have a bottle of their famous local cider. Do you allow this?

192 Following a rain delay, the batsman notices the bowler, who has taken two wickets, is drying the ball on a piece of cloth different to the one originally approved by the umpires. The bowler explains that the original cloth got too wet and he is using a piece of cloth he discovered in his pocket from a previous match. What is your decision?

After defending a delivery, a batsman leans over to pick up the ball so he can toss it to a nearby fielder. But as he does so, the non-striker calls him through for a single. He takes his hand off the ball, which is still on the ground, and completes the run. Do you intervene?

193

194

A batsman's drive flies right at you and without thinking you catch it. What happens next?

195

A legal delivery hits a batsman's boot well outside the line of the leg stump. As it bounces up, the batsman hits it for six. What do you do?

Two fast bowlers are repeatedly beating the bat. The wicketkeeper's glovework is faultless, and he appeals at every opportunity. The two struggling batsmen complain that the excessive appeals by the wicketkeeper are unacceptable and are affecting their concentration. What action do you take?

197

196

198

In a village match, the local favourite, a portly 60-year-old who has been playing for the team for over 40 years, asks you if, between overs and possibly during one or two of the overs being bowled, he can sit in a small collapsible chair the other side of the boundary rope. Do you agree to this?

A batsman plays the ball onto his wicket. It disturbs one bail, which does not fall but becomes lodged between the two stumps. Out or not out?

199

In a Twenty20 match, the bowler starts his run up when each new batsman arrives at the crease. Just before the delivery stride, he checks then walks back and starts again. The batsmen complain this is gamesmanship on the bowler's part and the abortive run ups are to see the intentions in the run chase of the new batsman. What action do you take?

200

201

A bowler is repeatedly hitting the batsman's pads. Although he appeals each time, he has failed to get even one LBW decision. You begin to suspect that under his breath the bowler is muttering disparaging remarks about your eyesight as he walks past you. What action do you take?

During his delivery stride, a bowler can see that the non-striker is well out of his crease, so he throws at the wicket in an attempted run out. But the ball misses the stumps and the batsmen race for a quick single. Does the run count?

The batting team need six runs off the last delivery to win. The batsman hits what looks like a certain six, but as it flies towards the boundary, a fielder throws his cap into the air and manages to stop it. Do you award five penalty runs or do you give the six, and therefore victory to the batting side?

203

202

The home team's main sponsor, a local car dealer, wants to drive the incoming batsmen to the crease in a branded convertible. The groundsman has agreed, but the opponents are not happy. Do you intervene?

204

A batsman is clean bowled, but you called no ball just as the delivery was unleashed. The fielding captain is angry and demands a review, insisting the batsman is out because your no ball decision was wrong. What happens now?

To ensure his side do not forget which side of the ball to polish, the captain has written the word 'shiny' on the new ball. An opposing batsman spots this, claiming it is ball tampering, and threatens to walk off. What do you do?

205

A batsman edges a delivery to first slip. Thinking he has been caught, he sets off for the pavilion, not spotting the slip fumble and drop the ball. Before he can regain his ground, the slip recovers the ball and runs him out. What now?

206

207

In a village match, a bowler completes a hat-trick and the No. 11 batsman is not ready to come into bat. After scrambling around picking up his pads and other equipment, he strides out to the middle just inside the two minutes. Once at the crease he sits down and finishes getting ready, strapping on both pads. The rival captain says he should be timed out. Is he right?

The ball is running towards the boundary rope in a village match. The crowd bursts into laughter as a golden retriever comes onto the field, picks up the ball, races off back over the boundary rope, and drops the ball at the feet of a small boy holding the lead from which the dog escaped. Do you signal dead ball when the dog picks up the ball, or do you wait until the dog has carried the ball over the rope and signal a boundary four?

209

208

The batsman attempts a defensive stroke, but only offers up a simple catch to a fielder who drops it. The batsman laughs at his good luck, but the fielder takes offence and hurls the ball straight back to the wicketkeeper, forcing the batsman to duck quickly to avoid being hit. The batsman leaves his crease and advances aggressively towards the fielder. What action do you take?

210

The fielding captain, unhappy with the catches dropped during the morning play, decides to cut short his team's lunch interval for some extra practice on the outfield. He asks you if they can use the match ball. What is your decision?

Dark clouds indicate rain is fast approaching. The fielding side, hanging on for a draw, are unnecessarily slow at the change of each over and the two bowlers are changing the field placing after almost every ball. The batsmen complain about the blatant time wasting. The fielding side insist they do not intend to be put under pressure because of the threatening weather. What action do you take?

The away captain wins the toss and notifies the home captain and the umpires of his decision to field. But as they start to walk off the field in preparation for the start of play, he realises he meant to say that he wanted to bat. Do you allow him to change his decision?

The players and officials are leaving the field at the end of play when you discover a mistake in the scoring that gave victory to the home team in error. The match is in fact a draw. What do you do?

The captain of the fielding team is a recognised world-class slip fielder. Following a rain delay, the grass and ball are wet. So are the hands of the captain, who has dropped two reasonable catches. The captain shows his wet hands to you and insists playing conditions are unfair and asks you to reconsider your decision to continue play. What do you do?

214

215

216

A batsman unintentionally fails to make good his ground. The batsmen turn and complete another run. Should you judge both runs as short runs, or should you award only the second run?

In a village match, the boundary mark is a two-inch wide white line. The home captain insists the ball must travel over the white line for it to count as a four. The away captain maintains that contact with the edge of the line nearest the pitch is sufficient for a four. Who is right?

The ball has been hit deep into the outfield and is heading for a certain boundary four. The two sprightly young batsmen at the crease are exceptionally fast and by the time the ball has crossed the boundary rope, they have clocked up a total of five runs. Do you give a boundary four or award five runs to the batsman?

217

218

You call a no ball, which is also wide. Do you add one or two runs to the batting team's total?

219

You call and signal a wide ball, which hits a close-to-the-wicket fielder and then rebounds to the batsman, who hammers it over the boundary for a four. Do you give one for the no ball, four to the batsman or award both – a total of five runs?

A batsman gets a top edge, sending the ball flying vertically upwards. He runs and crosses with his partner, but before the non-striker makes his ground, the ball lands in the crease and spins back onto the stumps. Is the striker bowled out or is the non-striker run out?

220

221

A batsman is hit by a delivery and drops his bat in pain. The bat breaks the wicket and fielders appeal. What now?

222

A fielder leaps high on the boundary to take a catch. As he lands holding the ball, both his feet are over the rope but off the ground. Do you signal a six or a catch.

The non-striking batsman is standing in his crease as the striker drives the ball hard towards the wicket at the bowler's end. The ball hits the base of the middle stump and rebounds back towards the striker's stumps. No one touches the ball, which dislodges the bails at the striker's end. The fielding team appeal that the striking batsman is out 'bowled' (played on). What is your decision?

225

223

A batsman plays a defensive shot. The ball bounces and spins sharply back towards the wicket. To avoid being bowled, the batsman hits the ball away, where it is caught by a close fielder. Is the batsman out?

224

A patch of outfield proved troublesome to mow and so the grass is longer than the rest of the field. A player takes a low catch, blades of grass clearly protruding between his hands and therefore making contact with the ball. There is no evidence that the ball has hit the 'ground'. Out or not out?

On a windy day during a village match, a batsman hits the ball straight back past the bowler and sets off for a run, when a large branch from an old tree overhanging the ground breaks loose and falls to the ground in the path of the ball and stops it. A fielder races over, picks up the ball and throws it to the wicketkeeper, who removes the bails and, with the batsman short of the crease, appeals. Out or not out?

228

226

A batsman made no attempt to hit a ball that caught the edge of his bat, flew past both the wicket and the wicketkeeper, and travelled over the boundary rope. What score do you award?

227

A fielder is experiencing discomfort from the new cricket shoes he is wearing. He asks you if he can go back into the dressing room and change shoes. He also asks if a substitute can come on and take his place while he is off the field. What is your decision?

229

You miscount the number of balls bowled and call over on the seventh ball, which is a wide. Does the single run awarded for the wide still count?

230

Your call of a wide ball is acknowledged by the batsman, who leans forward towards the ball, holding out his bat horizontally. The bat is well clear of the ball, but the batsman's back foot removes the bail. The wicketkeeper appeals. Out or not out?

231

In an attempted run out at the bowler's end, the ball knocks down all three stumps. The batsmen, having made their ground, see the ball has travelled into the outfield and set off for another run. The bowler manages to put the middle stump back into the ground. The fielder's throw removes the stump with the batsman out of his crease. What is your decision?

A batsman is racing to complete a quick single. He dives to make his ground, but his bat flies loose, away from the crease. However, he manages to stretch the hand that was holding the bat over the crease before the fielder's throw breaks the wicket. Out or not out?

232

233

234

An injured batsman plays the ball in the air, giving a fielder an excellent chance to take the catch. But the injured batsman's runner is in the way and refuses to move. The ball lands safely on the ground. What is your decision?

The batting captain is furious at what he considers blatant time wasting by the opposition. After an unnecessarily long over, he loses his cool and stands in the middle of the pitch, angrily calling on you to put a stop to it. What action do you take?

236

During the afternoon session of a game, one umpire gives a number of dubious decisions including two LBWs, resulting in the loss of three wickets. At the tea break, the captain spots the umpire drinking from a flask. When you, the second umpire, approach him, he smells strongly of alcohol. What happens now?

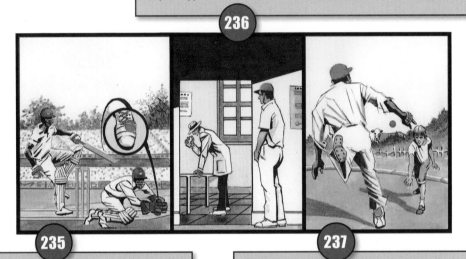

235

A batsman plays a defensive shot that hits the top of his boot and loops up. Realising that it is going to drop onto his wicket, he swots the ball away with his bat. The wicketkeeper catches the ball and appeals. Out or not out?

237

A batsman cover-drives the ball, which stops short of the rope. A young boy runs onto the field and throws the ball back to the chasing fielder, who whips the ball back to the wicketkeeper. The batsmen are denied a second easy run. What now?

239

On a sunny day, the batting captain, who is at the crease, points out that the watch on the bowling arm of the slow bowler should be removed because the sun reflecting off the watchface is proving a distraction. What is your decision?

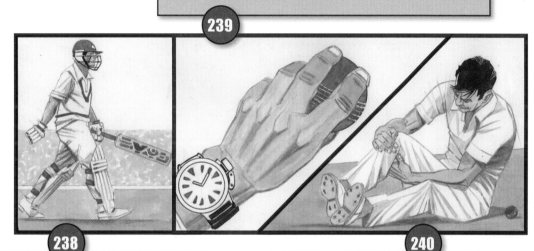

238

The global superstar of the home team strides to the wicket with the blade of his bat covered in commercial advertising. What action do you take?

240

It's the first day of a three-day match. Bowling the fifth ball in the final over, the bowler pulls up in his delivery stride with a hamstring injury. Do you signal a short-ball over or allow another bowler to step in and bowl the last two balls? Or do the fielders start the next day with a two-ball over?

The striking batsman, who has never scored a century, is on 99. He hits the ball into the outfield and his batting partner sets off for a quick single. The striking batsman is run out and, in his frustration, knocks all three stumps out of the ground. What is your decision?

242

241

Following an off-the-field incident in a previous match, there is bad feeling between the two captains. The home captain has requested that another member of his team attends the toss. Do you allow this?

243

A batsman takes the first step for a quick single, but he immediately realises he has made a mistake. He stops out of his crease and turns as the wicketkeeper collects the fielder's throw, removes the bails, and appeals. Is the batsman out 'stumped' or run out?

In a village match, the wicketkeeper has his injured little finger taped to the finger next to it for support. But when he takes an amazing catch, opponents protest, claiming the tape is loose and the sticky side helped trap the ball in his glove. Out or not out?

245

244

A batsman hammers the ball down the pitch. It travels at head height before making contact with the raised bat of the non-striker, who had turned away to avoid being hit. The bowler dives, catches the rebound, and appeals. Out or not out?

246

As a fielder slides to stop the ball on the boundary, his foot pushes the rope back. It isn't repositioned, and a few balls later, a batsman skids to the same area. The fielder holds the catch, but with one foot beyond where the rope originally would have been. Do you give a six or call out?

An exceptionally fast young bowler is repeatedly hitting the batsman's pads, but you have rejected his LBW appeals. Before starting his next over, the bowler asks you if your decisions are because the ball is going wide of the wicket or because it is going over the top of the stumps. Do you advise the bowler?

249

247

At the end of an end-of-season championship-deciding match, the umpires have agreed the scores with the scorers. But just as they start to leave the ground, one of the scorers spots a mistake. Can the result be changed?

248

Following a rain delay, you and your fellow umpire have made two inspections and decided the conditions are still not fit for play. The two captains, keen to start, ask if they can join you on your next inspection. What is your response?

On a windy day, the bowler takes off his jumper and hands it to you. You tie the sleeves of the jumper around your neck. The batsman is clean bowled on the next ball, but complains that the sleeves of the jumper were flapping around wildly and had distracted him. Is he out?

251

250

In a closely run match and with the batting side scoring freely, the captain of the fielding side asks you if he can dispense with his wicketkeeper. He wants to use him as an additional fielder instead – minus his gloves and pads. Do you allow this?

252

A bowler delivers a high-speed no ball. As it hurtles towards the wickets, the striker gets an inside edge attempting a straight drive, and the ball squirts back towards the wicket. The striker instinctively takes one hand off the bat and swats the ball away. There is an appeal. What now?

On the first day of a four-day match, you congratulate the head groundsman and his staff on the magnificent condition of the playing field. On the second day, the head groundsman informs you that in his opinion the grass did not need mowing, but all the creases have been re-marked. Has the groundsman overstepped his authority?

254

253

The No. 11 batsman is leading a charmed life much to the annoyance of the fast bowler. There is an exchange of words between the two and the next ball bowled is a full pitch above waist height aimed directly at the No. 11 who, but for his evasive action, would have been hit. The bowler holds up his hand in apology. What next?

255

A vicious no-ball bouncer forces the batsman to take a step back as the ball flies over his head. He immediately sets off for a run. As he does so, his bat knocks a stump and a bail falls. Is the batsman out?

The opening batsman plays the ball and races for a quick single. But the tail-ender remains in his crease and is joined by the opening batsman as the wicketkeeper collects the throw, which removes the bails. The tail ender leaves the crease and keeps walking until off the field. Is the opening bat still in? What is your decision?

257

256

258

You call and signal a wide ball, but the batsman has leaped out of this crease, getting the toe end of his bat on the ball, which goes over the boundary rope. Is it one run for the wide plus a boundary four, and is the batsman credited with the boundary?

A bowler has hit the batsman's pads twice without appeal. Both times you would have given the batsman out 'LBW'. In the next over, the bowler hits the batsman's pads – again without appeal – and again you would have ruled LBW. In the spirit of the game, would you have a quiet word with the bowler?

The fielding team are on the way to winning the match when heavy rain stops play. The next morning, the last day of the match, the sun is shining. After several ground inspections with the two captains, it is clear that part of the square is still unfit. The fielding captain, eager to start, insists that he will take responsibility if any player is injured because of the conditions. What do you do?

260

259

A batsman plays a defensive shot in front of his wicket. The ball hits his pad but you hear a noise that you think was an edge. The ball is caught by a fielder. Do you give the batsman out 'caught' or 'LBW'?

261

The opening batsman is partnered by the No. 10 with 6 runs needed for victory. The No. 10 hits the ball straight up into the air and sets off for a quick single. The close-to-the wicket fielder is faced with an easy catch, but instead of holding onto the ball, he directs it onto the stumps before the opening batsman makes his ground. Who is out?

The batting side need six runs to win off the last ball. The batsman makes a strike that is heading for a six, but a fielder positioned under the flight of the ball takes off his boot and hurls it at the ball, making contact inside the boundary. The batsmen, who had not bothered to run, watch as he makes the catch and returns the ball to the wicketkeeper. What is your decision?

262

263

264

A batsman drops his bat while running. He carries on and makes good his ground, then immediately turns and walks back along the pitch to retrieve his bat. At that moment, the wicketkeeper breaks the wicket and appeals. Out or not out?

A batsman plays a defensive shot to a good-length fast ball, which drops at his feet. As the fielders are deep in the slips and gully, the batsman picks up the ball with the bat still in his hand and lobs it back to the bowler. There is an appeal. What next?

The wicketkeeper collects the fielder's throw well behind the wicket and removes the bails. But the heel of the keeper's left foot is slightly behind the stumps while the rest of his foot is in front of the stumps. Is the batsman out or not out?

265

266

267

Before the start of play, the captain of the fielding side and the two opening bowlers have inspected the pitch. They inform you that they have decided there is to be no sweeping of the pitch and any surface clearance is to be performed by hand. Are they able to make this decision?

You have already called over when the bowler tells you he and the wicketkeeper are both convinced that on the last ball of the over the batsman was LBW. You agree, but do you allow this late appeal?

A batsman plays a defensive stroke to a slow spin bowler. The ball drops at his feet. The batsman then nonchalantly knocks the ball away with the side of his foot. The ball rolls straight back to the bowler, who picks it up and appeals. What is your decision?

In a one-day, two-innings village match, the away team rattle up 142. The home team are skittled for 62. The away captain asks the home captain to follow on, but the home captain insists you have to be 100 behind before you can enforce the follow on. The away captain is convinced it's 75 runs in a one-day match. Who is right?

The batsman plays forward and the ball strikes both the bat and the pad simultaneously. Half the ball strikes the bat, the other half the pad. The bowler and wicketkeeper appeal. Out or not out?

In a village match, a batsman who was a practising barrister, is annoyed to be given out and expertly argues his case at length with you and your fellow umpire. After several minutes of courtroom dramatics, he finally accepts your ruling and leaves the field. His replacement runs onto the field to take guard, only for the fielding captain to appeal for him to be given out 'timed out'. Five minutes have passed since you raised your finger to give the previous batsman out. What do you do now?

271

A spinner bowls a ball that hits the stumps and makes one of the bails jump. The wicketkeeper, seeing that there is a possibility that it will rest back in the grooves, swipes the bail away, making it fall to the ground, and then appeals. Is the batsman out?

272

In a village match, a batsman edges the ball. It is about to bounce just in front of first slip when a mole burrows up out of the outfield and the ball bounces on the unfortunate creature's head into the hands of the fielder who appeals for a catch. What is your decision?

With the light fading fast, a bowler changes ends after every over (he does not bowl two consecutively), and takes an unnecessary amount of time with the field placing, before each over. The two top-order batsmen, who are a few runs from victory, request that you stop the bowler from repeatedly changing ends. What do you do?

274

275

276

When they see the ball going straight to a fielder, both batsmen deliberately run a short run. But the fielder misfields and the ball goes for a boundary. Do you give a penalty for the deliberate short run, or award four to the batting side?

A bowler, hurrying to get in another over before close of play, sees the ball from the defensive stroke played by the batsman has stopped at your feet. To save time, the bowler asks you to pick it up and throw it back to him. Do you oblige?

On the last ball of the innings, the batting side need four runs to win. As the bowler starts his delivery, the striker slips and falls. The ball goes wide, with four wides scored. The fielding captain claims that the bowler was distracted. What do you do?

277

Taking a catch, a fielder passes the ball from one hand to the other several times, but then drops the ball to the ground. The batsman claims he is not out, but the fielder insists he had complete control before the ball dropped. Out or not out?

279

278

It is the final ball of the match and the two teams are level. The batsman is hit on the pad as he races off to get the single to win the match. After a moment's consideration you give him out 'LBW'. The fielding side celebrate, but the two batsmen, having completed the single, refer the LBW decision to the third umpire. The decision is reversed and the batting side claim victory. The fielding side insist that the wicketkeeper could have picked up the ball and easily run out the batsman had they attempted a single with a not out decision. What is your ruling?

A very popular former test cricket captain, having announced he will retire from playing cricket at the end of this one-day match, walks to the crease for the last time. The batsman hits the first ball he receives straight back to the bowler, who instinctively takes a clean catch, but sportingly he does not appeal, instead he turns still holding the ball and walks back to bowl the next delivery. Do you intervene?

280

281

It's Winston Churchill's birthday, and a cricketer always smokes a huge Churchillian cigar to mark the occasion. Unfortunately, five quick wickets fall and the cigar-smoking opening batsman's team are all out. Defiantly still smoking the huge cigar, the cricketer walks out to field. Do you permit this?

282

A fast bowler, unable to dismiss the No. 11 batsman, loses his temper and starts to bowl each delivery fairly, but short-pitched and straight at the batsman, not at the stumps. What action do you take?

284

A batsman walks after you give him out 'LBW'. But as he goes, you spot a bail lying on the ground. You are sure it wasn't dislodged by the batsman or a fielder, and you are aware that the wicket was re-made by the fielding side after it was broken on the previous delivery. What do you do now?

283

A batsman aborts a run and trots back behind the crease. But the non-striker keeps running, shouting at his colleague, who ignores him. With both batsmen now behind the same crease, a fielder knocks down the wicket at the bowler's end. Who is out?

285

With dark storm clouds gathering, there is a sudden loud crack of thunder and a flash of lightning as the ball beats the bat and splinters the stumps. The batsman shakes his head and points his finger skywards. What is your decision?

A fielder collapses with a torn hamstring while chasing a ball that has stopped just short of the boundary rope. Do you signal dead ball, allow the batsmen to complete their fourth run then signal dead ball, or allow play to continue?

286

Facing the first ball after lunch, a batsman has mistakenly left his phone in his pocket. It suddenly rings and a startled fielder drops an easy catch. What action do you take?

288

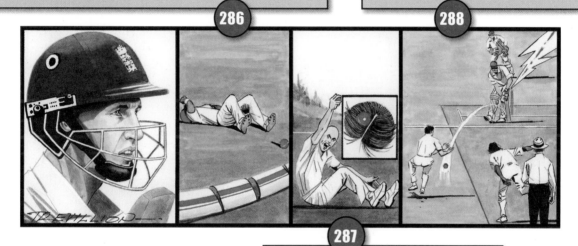

287

A fielder's wig flies off as he fumbles a high catch. But seeing the ball drop onto his wig on the grass, he picks it up and appeals. Out or not out?

A batsman has been given out 'caught'. However, the fielder who made the catch has been informed the ball touched the ground first and now wishes to withdraw the appeal. The batsman has just left the field of play, but the incoming batsman has still not walked onto the field of play. What do you do?

290

289

Your fellow umpire is portly with a small moustache and you are short and thin. As you both walk out, you are greeted by the crowd, singing the Laurel and Hardy signature tune, which they repeat every time a decision goes against the home team. Both captains suggest this is beginning to affect your decisions. How do you respond?

291

A batsman, who has twice been hit on his helmet, ducks into another high ball, misjudges the bounce and, putting up his hand, instinctively catches the ball. He walks down the pitch still holding the ball and drops it at the bowler's feet. What next?

A gust of wind catches the batsman's cap and blows it onto the bails, dislodging them just as he swipes the ball to the boundary. There is an appeal. What now?

292

A young batsman completes the run that will give him his first century. As he makes good his ground, he leaps in the air to celebrate just as a fielder hurls the ball at the wicket. The fielders appeal. What now?

294

293

A fast bowler with an aggressive on-field reputation delivers a ball that hits the striker on the pads. The bowler appeals. The umpire says not out. Unhappy with the decision, the bowler asks the umpire why he did not give the batsman out. When the umpire answers, the bowler responds by angrily pushing the umpire to the ground. As the umpire lies flat on his back in some pain, a fielder who has been on the boundary, races up and abuses the umpire, blaming him for the unpleasant event. What now?

After hitting a string of sixes, a batsman is surprised when the ball suddenly starts to swing and is caught at slip. As the fielders celebrate, a spectator storms on. He alleges that when the last six was fired into the stand, the fan who caught it spat on the ball and rubbed it furiously on his trousers before tossing it back. What do you do?

296

295

A slow bowler spots a confident batsman edging out of his crease. So before entering his delivery stride, he hurls the ball at the striker's stumps and appeals. Out or not out?

297

The batsmen complete four runs before a fielder manages to hurl the ball back towards the wicketkeeper. But the ball doesn't reach him. Instead, it hits the keeper's helmet, lying on the grass, and deflects back out over the boundary rope. How many runs are scored?

You are at the bowler's end and the match is about to start. The batsman has been informed where his middle stump is, and the officials and all the fielding players have clearly indicated they are ready. However, you forget to shout 'play'. The bowler runs up and delivers a fair ball that removes the bails. The batsman claims he wasn't ready because he didn't know the game had started. What now?

298

299

300

In the last over of a tense match, the home side need one run to win and the visitors need one wicket to fall. During the over, the batsman plays the ball two feet in front of him and races for a quick single, but collides with the bowler. Both are injured and neither can continue. What do you do?

A wicketkeeper anticipates a run out, so he drops his glove ready to collect the ball and hurl it at the stumps. But his on-target throw hits the glove instead, which in turn dislodges the bails. Out or not out?

THE ANSWERS

Page 20

1 Consult your colleague, leave the field of play and ask the batting captain why the incoming batsman was not ready to face the next ball, or for his colleague to do so. If his answer is unacceptable, give the incoming batsman out 'timed out'.

The former Lancashire opener Andrew Kennedy was given out timed out while playing for Dorset in a Minor Counties match. Kennedy was next in, but had gone to the toilet and not informed his team-mates. A wicket fell, and when he did not appear, he was given out on appeal.

2 There is nothing in the laws that prohibits a player from wearing boots or shoes with advertising logos. However, the umpire must know if the playing conditions of the competition allow advertising on equipment, in which case you may need to take action.

3 Your ruling should be out 'caught', because the ball did not strike the ground.

Page 21

4 This is a case of illegal fielding. The moment the ball strikes the book, you should call and signal dead ball. Award five penalty runs to the batting side, plus two runs to the striker. Do not count the ball in that over and report the fielder.

5 When the run is completed, call and signal dead ball, cancel the run, and return the batsmen to their original ends. Because no stroke has been offered, no runs can be scored. Had the ball been caught, you would have given the striker out on appeal. By allowing the first run, you give the fielders the chance to get a run out.

6 The fielding captain is wrong and you should award four runs. The sole reason that the ball did not touch the boundary rope is that the fielder had pushed it away. In any event, a line would be visible on the grass where the rope had been, and therefore the line cannot be judged to have moved.

Page 22

7 Yes, the second run does count because the collision with the bat and ball was accidental.

8 No, you do not. The laws do not restrict the choice of footwear.

9 You should call out 'hit wicket'. The handkerchief must be considered part of his clothing or equipment. The situation is the same as if part of his bat had broken off on contact with the ball and had broken the wicket.

Page 23 Moeen Ali

10 If the ball did not hit the ground after leaving the bat, you should award six runs, otherwise award four. In either case, the batting side win with one ball remaining.

11 No. Because the wicketkeeper was not injured, he cannot have a substitute. Another fielder can take up the gloves.

12 None. For the batsman to be out 'hit the ball twice', the second strike must be clearly intentional. But bear in mind whenever applying this law that the batsman is allowed to hit the ball twice in defending his wicket. This means that if the ball were rebounding onto his wicket after the first strike or off his person, he would be able to hit it a second time. However, he cannot do so if this would prevent a catch from being taken.

Page 24

13 The correct call on appeal is out 'run out'. The umpire is deemed to be part of the field of play and a batsman can be caught from a deflection off the umpire.

14 Unless there is an appeal from the fielding captain, you should allow the run. This scenario happens on a regular basis throughout the cricket world, where with one run to win and the match lost, the fielding captain does not insist that the batsmen at the crease ground their bats to complete the win. Cricket is a game of great traditions and this is one of them.

15 Both tennis and cricket are played to their own laws and regulations. What is permissible on the tennis court is not necessarily so on the cricket field. While a tennis player is allowed to change an item of clothing on court, in cricket the only place for changing clothing is the changing room. An attempt by a batsman to change shirt at the wicket is likely to be viewed as a time-wasting ploy and would not be allowed.

Page 25

16 Tell the captain to get on with his job. The umpires are the only judges of fair and unfair play. If the bowler needs a dressing for an obvious injury, this should be permitted. You're not a doctor, and neither is the captain.

The notion that having a plaster on the finger of the bowling hand gives a bowler an unfair advantage is a fallacy. In fact, it interferes with the grip on the ball, thereby reducing control.

17 It cannot be a six because the ball had been on the ground. The runs completed before the fielder picked up the ball should be awarded, plus the four for hitting the tree branch.

18 Because the striker's end umpire deliberately caught the ball, his colleague should immediately call and signal dead ball, so no runs can be scored nor wickets taken. Had the ball struck one of the umpires and, without hitting the ground, been caught by a fielder, the striker should be called out on appeal.

Page 26 Hashim Amla

19 Sadly for the striker, he is run out on appeal if he has not made his ground. The fact that the ball hit his helmet changes nothing; the ball is still live. Similarly, if it had come off his bat and then hit the helmet while playing a stroke, and the ball was subsequently caught, he would also be out.

20 Call and signal no ball. In the past, at all levels, bowlers routinely broke the non-striker's wicket. In my 27 years of umpiring, I never heard of or saw a batsman complaining of being distracted in this way. However, some years ago in a test match between England and South Africa at Headingley, both Smith and Kallis complained about Finn repeatedly breaking the wicket. The umpire had little option but to call and signal dead ball, although it did look strange when Smith and Kallis hit balls to the boundary. In my view, this complaint should not arise; during delivery batsmen should be watching the bowler's hand, not the wicket.

21 The bowler's end umpire should immediately call and signal dead ball. The action of the non-striker in catching the ball was instinctive. He was trying to avoid injury, which he was entitled to do.

Page 27

22 It definitely is quick thinking, but it's not very clever. As soon as the ball lodges in the batsman's clothing or equipment you must call and signal dead ball. It would be grossly unfair for the batting side to be able to score runs in this way, while the fielding side were denied the chance to take a wicket. In any case, for a six to be awarded, the ball must come off the bat, not off the batsman's person.

23 Yes, the wicketkeeper has been lucky here. There was no stumping, but the ball never landed on the ground after hitting the batsman's wicket, so the catch stands.

24 The correct call is out 'hit wicket'. If in receiving or preparing to receive a delivery, the striker breaks his wicket, he must be given out on appeal.

Page 28 Jimmy Anderson

25 No. The fielder must keep hold of the ball and be in control of his further movement. In this instance, as soon as the players collide, call and signal dead ball. This is especially important when there is a clash of heads, resulting in a potentially serious injury. Once dead ball has been called, nothing else can happen, so a wicket cannot be taken nor runs scored.

26 Call dead ball and consult your colleague. Then issue a first and final warning to the captain of the fielding side. If time-wasting continues, award five penalty runs every time there is a transgression. Ban the bowler if it happens during an over. If it happens between overs, ban the person who bowled the last over. Report the matter to the authorities.

27 You should call out 'run out for obstruction', if in your opinion the batsman deliberately changed direction and ran into the path of the ball.

A similar situation arose in 2013 in a One-Day International between Pakistan and South Africa. There was a mix-up in calling for a second run between two Pakistan top-order batsmen. As Hafeez, the non-striker, ran towards the bowler's end, he suddenly changed direction, ran in front of the wicket, and was struck by the ball. The South Africans appealed and, after the umpires conferred, Hafeez was given out 'for obstruction'.

Page 29

28 You should respond to the fielder's petulant behaviour by awarding eight runs to the striker – four that were run, plus four for the ball thrown over the boundary. The fielding captain will not be amused by this expensive display of temper by his team-mate.

29 As soon as the boy steps onto the field of play and touches the ball, you or your colleague should call and signal dead ball to prevent any further development. You should then decide how many runs should be awarded to the batting side. In this case, it looks as if this would have been a certain boundary, so you should award four.

30 One of the many things umpires need to do before play starts is to supervise the toss, which should take place no more than 30 minutes and no less than 15 minutes before the scheduled start of play. Whatever time the umpires arrive, they must insist on witnessing the toss in order to prevent this embarrassing situation.

Page 30 Jonny Bairstow

31 Not out. Obstruction must be seen to be intentional, and in this instance it clearly was not. Immediately call and signal dead ball.

32 The striker remains on 96 because as soon as no ball is called, one run is automatically credited to the batting side and the match is over.

There have been incidents like this in bad-tempered matches where, to prevent the opponent from getting a hundred, the bowler has deliberately bowled a wide or no ball. This is not against the laws but against the spirit of the game.

33 Not out. In a county match, if a high bouncer is bowled from which a batsman cannot play a normal shot, the bowler's end umpire should call and signal no ball, so the batsman cannot then be caught. However, had this been an international match, a special playing condition would have applied, whereby a very high bouncer is called a wide. But in this case, because the striker has hit the ball, wide could not have been called, so he would be given out 'caught' on appeal.

Page 31

34 You should give the striker out 'bowled'. The non-striker returns to the bowler's end, so that the incoming batsman takes strike. Had there been a run out, the new batsman would not be on strike. The length of time that the ball is in the air is irrelevant.

35 Take no action. There is absolutely nothing in the laws of cricket that prohibits a player receiving instructions or coaching from the sidelines, even via this kind of technology.

36 The batsman is out 'run out'. The red handkerchief does not look anything like a ball and is not even close to it. Players and umpires should all watch the ball and be aware of where it is at all times.

Page 32

37 Give out 'for obstructing the field'. This used to be out 'handle ball', but this new ruling is one of the recent law changes. In the Ashes Test at Old Trafford in 1993 when Graham Gooch knocked away a ball that had come off his body and was about to drop onto his wicket, umpire Dickie Bird gave him out 'handle ball' on appeal.

38 This complaint is frivolous and should be dismissed. The comments are made between overs and are in no way abusive or disrespectful. This cannot be said to break anyone's concentration.

39 Do nothing, but when the time for close of play has been reached, call time and inform the scorers and both teams that the match was a draw. Even when a striker has been bowled, there must be an appeal. There is no such thing as an automatic dismissal.

Page 33

40 Take tea and complete the match afterwards, weather allowing. You can be flexible in these situations if both sides agree to delay an interval. However, clearly in this case the two teams have competing agendas; the batting side want to win the match quickly before the rain comes, while the fielding side will want to take tea on time, hoping for a downpour that washes out the rest of the day, thus ensuring a draw. So simply follow the laws to avoid argument.

41 There is nothing in the laws to stop them from doing this, as long as they do not do it on any part of the square or cause unacceptable damage to the outfield. You should allow practice catching to go ahead.

42 Call dead ball, consult your colleague and speak to the fielding captain. Tell the latter that bowling the ball into the rough area is illegal and must stop as it will alter the condition of the ball.

Page 34 Stuart Broad

43 The correct call is out 'bowled'. The ball is still live and the striker did not tread on his wicket, so it cannot be 'hit wicket'.

44 It would be in order to play on. The stumps are of regulation dimensions as the law specifies. There is no need to use branded equipment. The home team should be congratulated for their ingenuity.

45 You have to give not out. This is really quick thinking by the batsman, who clearly knew the law.

Page 35 Jos Buttler

46 As soon as the bowler stops in his run up, you should call and signal dead ball. But if you have not seen it, consult your colleague, who is in a much better position to see what happened. You then accept their final decision. If the bowler's action was judged unfair, give the batsman not out, then give the bowler a warning. Otherwise, give the batsman out 'bowled'.

47 The batsman is out 'run out' on appeal. Had the ball deflected off the bat and run into the outfield, the batsmen could have continued completing more runs or gone over the boundary for four overthrows.

48 This is blatant time wasting, which you cannot tolerate. Give the fielding side's captain a first and final warning, and inform the batsmen too. If there is any repeat of the time wasting, either you or your colleague should call and signal dead ball. In addition, if the time wasting takes place during an over, instruct the fielding captain to take the bowler off immediately, ruling he cannot bowl again in that innings. If it takes place in between overs, award five penalty runs to the batting side. Finally, report what happened to the relevant governing body.

Page 36

49 There are two issues here: time wasting and the safety of all concerned. Award five penalty runs to the batting side for the bowler's time wasting. You might request that he be taken off from bowling. On the issue of potential danger to the batsmen, you will need to make a decision based on your own assessment of the conditions.

50 Under the new laws, you must give out 'for obstructing the field'. Having played the ball once, the striker has no right to intercept wilfully the ball except in protecting himself.

51 No runs are scored. Give the batsman out on appeal. He is allowed only one chance to hit the ball. After it came off his body, he should not have deliberately struck it. The striker is allowed to hit the ball only twice in defending his wicket, and as long as in so doing he does not prevent a catch from being taken.

Page 37

52 No, the bowler is wrong and the batsman is not out. The bails must be removed entirely from the top of the wicket for the striker to be bowled. In this case they are not.

53 You must give out 'run out'. Because the fielder had touched the ball, the striker cannot be stumped, even though the wicket was broken by the wicketkeeper. A stumping can only be effected by the wicketkeeper with no involvement from a fielder.

54 Out LBW. The appeal must be made before the bowler starts his run up for the start of next over. In this case the appeal was made in time.

Page 38 Alastair Cook

55 No action is needed. Any player can wear as much padding under his clothing as he likes. The law only deals with external equipment. At First Class and international level, fielders routinely wear shin pads and other items of protective equipment. The only fielder who can wear external pads is the wicketkeeper.

56 Before the match starts the umpires have certain duties to perform, two of which are to define the boundaries to both captains and inform them what action they would take if a spectator or animal entered the field of play and came into contact with the ball which was in play. Normally in this situation you would immediately call and signal dead ball, then award a boundary if you thought the ball would have gone to the boundary. If not, award the runs completed before the interception. In this case, it seems that you should award a boundary six.

57 Give the non-striker out 'run out'. The non-striker cannot lawfully leave his ground until the bowler is into his delivery swing. Also, there is no compulsion for the bowler to warn him.

The only reason for a non-striker to leave his ground early is to gain a few yards, which is blatantly unfair and illegal. A warning was given so there is no excuse for repeating the transgression.

Page 39

58 The bowler must tell the umpire if he is bowling left- or right-handed and whether over or around the wicket. The umpire will then inform the striker. The bowler can change the ball from left to right, but must deliver the ball as he told the umpire.

59 As soon as you see the fielder take the ball out of his pocket, you should call and signal dead ball. Instruct the fielding captain to ensure that the ball is immediately removed from the field of play.

60 Whatever clothing or equipment he was wearing is part of his person. If in receiving or preparing to receive a legal delivery any part of that clothing or equipment breaks the wicket, he must be given out 'hit wicket' on appeal.

61 Your ruling must be based on which batsman was nearest to the wicket at the instant that it was broken. That player must be given out run out on appeal. If the two batsmen had crossed originally and had not crossed again before the wicket was put down, and the star man was nearer to that wicket, he is run out.

In the One-Day International between England and Australia at Lords, there was a mix-up between David Wade and his captain Michael Clarke. Wade pushed a ball towards mid-wicket, started to run, stopped and returned to his ground. But Clarke raced to the striker's end, making good his ground. As Clarke was batting well, Wade left his ground and allowed himself to be run out as the wicket at the bowler's end was put down.

62 As the umpire, your decision is final. Consult your fellow umpire, who might have seen exactly what happened and may confirm your ruling. A refusal to play is deemed to have occured if a batsman refuses to leave the field after being given out or if a team refuse to take the field. Tell the batsman his action will result in that team forfeiting the match, which will be awarded to the opposition. That should focus his mind.

63 As the striker's end umpire, you should call and signal no ball because the bowler threw the ball. The bowler's end umpire should then repeat the no ball signal to the scorers. The ball will not count in the over. Finally, you must give the striker out 'run out'. In these circumstances, a batsman can be given out even from a no ball. The bowler's quick thinking is rewarded.

64 Yes, you can permit this change. With permission from both umpires, the wicketkeeper can be replaced by a specialist substitute wicketkeeper.

65 Deliberate distraction is illegal. As the sole judge of fair and unfair play, based on what you see, you must decide if the wicketkeeper's action is unfair or not. If you judge the exaggerated movements of the wicketkeeper to be deliberate, you should give a warning.

66 On appeal, you should give out 'hit the ball twice'. The striker is allowed one chance to hit the ball. If the ball hits him, that is his one chance and he should leave the ball to the fielders. If he wilfully strikes it after being hit, he is guilty of hitting the ball twice. What's more, the runs from the strike will not count, so in this case you cannot award a boundary six.

Page 42

67 You do nothing. The bowler is not obliged to show the ball to the striker as he runs up. It is common to see bowlers covering the ball so that the striker cannot see how it is being gripped as this will give the latter a good idea as to how the ball will react after release.

68 This is great batting. Cricket is a battle of wits, and here the striker has clearly outwitted the bowler. Signal six.

69 Out 'for obstructing the field'. This would have been 'handle ball' before the recent law change. Once the striker has had his one strike at the ball, he must not touch or interfere with the ball, unless requested to do so by a member of the fielding side.

Page 43

70 Not out. Obstruction must be seen to be intentional. This applies to both the batting and fielding sides. Here the batsman set off in a straight line to reach his ground and the bowler went to field the ball. There was no deliberate obstruction.

71 Having given the striker out you can stick with your decision if you are convinced you were right. But in this case, I would call dead ball, signal to the scorers that I was revoking my decision and call not out and allow the batsman to resume his innings. Finally, I would thank the wicketkeeper for his honesty.

72 You are entitled to agree to this request if you judge that the conditions warrant the extra drinks interval. As the umpire, you have a duty of care to every player. This alone should determine your decision. The batsman has no say in the matter, and if he continues to complain should be charged with dissent.

Page 44

73 Yes, the batting team's captain is correct. There are two important factors here. A batsman can only be given out on appeal and here there was no appeal. Also, time had been called so the session had ended and everyone left the field to go to lunch. The call of time means that nothing further could happen during that period of play. However, the striker should be allowed to resume his innings when play resumes.

74 Yes, he is out. The runner is part of play and the ball never touched the ground. The catch is therefore fair.

75 The batsman is out 'caught'. The fact that he was not actually holding the bat as the ball struck it does not affect your decision. Great fast bowling.

76 As soon as the ball becomes enmeshed in the paper, you should call and signal dead ball. This means that nothing further can happen, and no catch can be awarded. The runs completed plus the run in progress if the batsmen have crossed will be awarded to the batting side.

77 There are 42 laws that govern the game of cricket at the highest levels, but there are also playing regulations, which supersede the laws. These often apply in village matches. The law says that only 11 players should take the field at any one time, but that the captains are entitled to field with more. This is clearly a fun match, so with the agreement of both sides, you can allow this increase in team numbers.

78 This is a case of illegal fielding and you should immediately call dead ball. Permission should have been sought from the umpires before the fielder re-entered the field of play. In addition, add five penalty runs to the batting side, rule that any runs scored or attempted will count and that the ball will not count in that over. After the match you should report the offending fielder to the authorities for that league.

79 Signal out 'caught'. The ball did not touch the ground and so it is still live.

80 You must insist that the incoming batsman remains on the field. The batsman's innings started as soon as he stepped onto the field of play, so the captain cannot call him back and send another batsman in. This would not apply if play had not been called at the start of a match. In this case, if the players and umpires have cause to leave the field, the opening batsmen can be replaced by two others who have been nominated.

81 No, the batsman cannot be bowled from a rebound off the wicketkeeper. But had he left his ground, he would have been out 'stumped'. Also he could have been out 'run out' if he had left his ground and attempted a run.

82 This is a valid decision. There is nothing in the laws that compels the striker's end umpire to stand on the leg side. The umpires should stand on the side that offers them the best view of what they need to see, and the umpires themselves are best qualified to make this choice.

83 Not out on appeal is the correct call. A striker can lawfully kick or knock away a ball that has landed and is rolling back onto his wicket. He cannot take a hand off the bat and knock the ball away with that hand.

84 The bowler's end umpire should instruct the non-striker to stand where he does not impede or obstruct members of the fielding side. This is a lawful instruction that must be obeyed. The non-striker cannot choose to stand on the side he likes.

Page 48

85 Yes, the batsman is right. The length of a pitch is 66 feet, so the interception is made 22 feet from the wicket, a distance that would make a call of LBW very unreliable. What's more, if the ball turns, swings or moves off the pitch, the more difficult it is to guess where it is likely to go. To give a batsman out under these circumstances would be an enormous guess and a diabolical decision. Not even the much-heralded Hawk-Eye could say that this ball would hit have the wicket.

86 This discussion is not permissable. The toss cannot take place more than 30 minutes or less than 15 minutes before the scheduled start. The umpires will tell the captain that he must inform his opponent immediately of his decision. The captain is not allowed to go away and chat with his team and coach first.

87 Even though many current and former players think it is unfair, the switch hit is legal and the boundary six stands.

Page 49

88 The striker is out 'caught' even though the wicket at the bowler's end was broken first. At no point did the ball touch the ground, so the catch takes precedence over the run out.

89 As soon as it is clear that a player is injured, one of the umpires should call and signal dead ball, so nothing else can happen. The game is drawn because the run was not completed. This is the fairest decision.

90 If the ball has just been returned to the bowler and is still live, you should give the non-striker out 'run out' because he is out of his ground. His bat is meant to be held in his hands, not sat on.

Page 50 M. S. Dhoni

91 Although you should have been more careful to count the number of balls, your decision is final. The seven-ball over cannot be changed, the batsman is out and neither side have any say on the matter.

92 Not out. You should call and signal dead ball. The fielder's shirt should be tucked into the waist of his trousers, not lying on the field of play. It would be grossly unfair to give the striker out in these circumstances.

93 If the red wristband is causing a distraction for the batsmen, you should instruct the bowler to take it off. Many years ago when I was bowling for Hampshire against Sussex, their batsman complained to the umpires that my shirt, which was open to my chest, was flapping as I ran up to the wicket and was distracting him. I was told to button up my shirt.

Page 51

94 A batsman can lawfully hit the ball a second time in defending his wicket. Additionally, the umpire would have to determine whether or not he knocked the ball away from the fielder intentionally.

95 That batsman can only face the next ball if the previous one was the last ball of an over and he is facing the first ball of the next. After the second transgression, call and signal dead ball, award five penalty runs to the fielding side, and return the batsmen to their original ends. The single does not count and you must report the offender to the relevant authority.

96 Award six runs to the striker because the ball came off the bat, then onto his boot and he did not intentionally kick the ball. The ball hit the batsman's boot as a result of him lifting his foot in playing the stroke.

Page 52

97 In this instance, you should rule that the over be completed by another member of the fielding side. That person cannot have bowled the previous over. In addition, in a limited overs match where bowlers are restricted to a set number of overs, that person must not have bowled his allowance of overs.

98 The home captain is wrong; you must allow this. If the late arrival is a nominated player, he can bat in whichever order his captain chooses.

99 Yes, he is out 'caught'. The fielder did not deliberately use his shirt to catch the ball. It was accidental.

One of the best short-leg fielders I ever saw was Basharat Hassan of Nottinghamshire. On several occasions he caught full-blooded pull shots. As he ducked and bent over, he folded his arms to his chest, and the ball lodged in his shirt, which had ballooned out. The catches were allowed.

Page 53 Mitchell Johnson

100 Not out. The bat was dropped accidentally so there can be no obstruction. What's more, the thrown ball must hit the wicket, not the bat lying on the ground. I would also call dead ball as soon as the ball strikes the bat.

101 Immediately call and signal dead ball and give the batsman not out. This is a ploy by the bowler to surprise the batsman, knowing that he is not ready. Inform his captain that this is unfair play and give the bowler a warning. You should also report the incident.

102 He has not made his ground. No part of the batsman's body or bat was grounded behind the popping crease when the wicket was thrown down. He is run out on appeal. However, the collision between him and the bowler was accidental. For this reason, the striker's end umpire could ask the fielding captain if he wants the appeal to stand. Should he say that he does, the batsman must be given out 'run out'. If it was clear that either the batsman or bowler had been injured during the collision, one of the umpires should call and signal dead ball. This prevents any further development, such as runs, wickets or controversy.

Page 54

103 According to a recent law change, your ruling must be not out and you should award six runs. For a catch to be lawful, the first touch must be made from the field of play. This means that the fielder can knock the ball up, run off the field, and then move back onto the field to take the catch. Another fielder may also take the catch.

Before the law change, there was an incident in a One-Day International when the Sri Lankan player Angelo Matthews, who was fielding on the boundary, backed off the field of play, jumped into the air, and knocked the ball back over the field of play. He then re-entered the field and caught the ball. The striker was given out 'caught'. This could not happen under the new law.

104 Give the striker out 'bowled'. It is the umpires who answer the appeals and run the match, not any player, and their decision is final.

105 In principle, yes. There's nothing in the laws that prevents a female playing in a match where the other players are male. The only factors that could be relevant are if there is a restriction imposed by the league in question that prohibits women from taking part in men's matches, or if there is a lack of suitable changing facilities.

Page 55 Brendon McCullum

106 You do nothing. There is no law against the bowling of wides or no balls. Their actions would be against the spirit of cricket and, as it is an international match, the ICC might intervene as there would likely be much criticism and controversy.

In this situation, I am certain that the subject of match fixing would raise its head, as it did in the Test match at Lords in 2010 when two Pakistani bowlers, Asif and Amir, were found guilty of deliberately bowling no balls for payment. Captain Salman Butt was also found guilty of complicity. All three were banned.

107 The striker is out 'caught'. The sunglasses and cap on the bowler's head are part of his dress.

108 No. The fielding captain has no authority to question what a player who is off the field does. That lies with the batting captain alone.

Page 56 Eoin Morgan

109 You may suspect that this is a ploy by the fielding side to upset the batsman, but I would consult my colleague and examine the bat. Unless there is some type of metallic coating on the bat, it's hard to believe that a piece of willow could be so shiny as to cause problems for the fielding side.

110 No. Give the batsman out 'run out'. You only need to dislodge the remaining bail from the stump to achieve a run out.

111 The home side are right. A captain who wants to enforce the follow-on must inform his opposite number as soon as his team's innings ends or he declares. There must be a ten-minute interval before the next innings starts. If adequate time is not given, the umpires will enforce the ten-minute interval. Any time lost is deducted from the remaining playing time.

This actually happened in an under 19 Test match in 1989 at Old Trafford, between England and New Zealand. England compiled a huge score, then bowled the New Zealanders out cheaply. Nick Knight, the home captain, told Barrie Meyer and me, the two umpires, as we left the field, he would enforce the follow-on. But we were not aware that he had not told his opposite number, Chris Cairns.

Five minutes later we walked out onto the field followed by both teams, ready to field. There was surprise on everyone's face. Nick Knight then told us he thought it was enough for him to inform the umpires, but we told him he had also to tell the opposing captain. Both teams returned to the pavilion and play started ten minutes late with New Zealand batting.

Page 57

112 If the collision is a heavy one and there is the likelihood of serious injury, you should immediately call and signal dead ball, thereby preventing any further development. If the collision is not a heavy one, play should be allowed to continue. It is highly unlikely that both batsmen lying on the ground will be completely level. As there cannot be two dismissals from the same delivery, the one nearest the wicketkeeper is out 'run out' on appeal.

113 In these circumstances, non-matching pads are permissable. The protection of the batsman from injury is of paramount importance. Therefore the batsman would be allowed to wear the white pad.

114 If the other bail is removed when the ball hits the wicket, the striker is out 'bowled' on appeal.

Page 58

115 Give the non-striker out 'for obstructing the field'. You should also report him to the relevant authorities for the illegal act.

116 Call and signal dead ball as soon as the striker recoils. The ball does not count and must be bowled again.

117 Yes, you should immediately call and signal dead ball. Players are not allowed to discard clothing or equipment by dropping it on the field. No runs can be scored from a dead ball.

Page 59 Kevin Pietersen

118 Give the batsman out 'run out'. The bat must be held in the hand, not simply have fingers resting on it.

119 This is a case of negligence by both umpires. On the call of time before the break, the umpire should take possession of the match ball and not leave it with the players. As things stand, you should replace it with another ball of similar wear. Award five penalty runs to the batting side. The player who bowled the last over should be banned from bowling for the rest of the innings. After the match he should be reported to the relevant authorities.

120 You and your fellow umpire should confer and decide if the non-striker's call distracted the fielder, causing him to pull out of the catch. If the non-striker's call is deemed to have caused obstruction, give the striker out. Award five penalty runs to the fielding side and the ball will not count in the over. Report the offender. No runs are scored. If the non-striker was not deemed to have obstructed the fielder, call and signal dead ball and re-bowl that delivery.

Page 60

121 You do not have to agree to help the bowler, but if allowing the practice run up and telling him where his front foot lands does not waste time, you can allow it. On the question of umpires helping players, a former Middlesex and England captain would always ask me to check if he was picking the bat up and bringing it down straight at the start of his innings, and I would tell him.

122 You cannot agree to the fielder's request. If he wants the wicket repaired, he must do it himself. As the ball is still live, be sure to position yourself to adjudicate on a possible run out. When the ball becomes dead, you can repair the wicket.

123 If you think the complaint is valid, you can suspend play and ask the ground authority to make an announcement over the public address system, which explains the batsmen's problem and asks for a reduction in the noise level from the crowd.

Page 61

124 Sadly, in this case, you are guilty of negligence. It is your duty to ascertain whether or not the bowler is going to bowl over or around the wicket and whether with the right or left arm. Umpires must train themselves to always do the basic fundamentals of the job. Fortunately for you, the striker did not complain. He would have been justified in pulling away.

125 The batsman is not out. As soon as the ball lands on the fielder's cap lying on the ground, you should call and signal dead ball, to prevent any further development. Had the cap not been there, the ball would have landed safely on the ground. It should also be noted that the fielder did not deliberately put his cap there, which would have been a case of illegal fielding, resulting in five penalty runs being awarded to the batting side.

126 The non-striker is out 'run out'. In any event, the bat he is touching is not his own. It is not sufficient for the hand to be resting on the bat handle. His fingers must be actually holding the handle to be lawful.

Page 62

127 Your decision stands. You and your colleague are the sole judges of fair and unfair play. Once the striker has been given out, any refusal to leave the field of play will be regarded as dissent. If the webbing on the wicketkeeper's gloves was illegal, you should have seen and dealt with it earlier.

128 You cannot allow practice to take place on or near the square and pitch. There is ample space to practise catching on the rest of the outfield. Doing so near the pitch and square will not improve their catching.

129 The bowler is entitled to change sides, as long as he informs the umpire beforehand, who will then tell the striker.

Page 63

130 This is an unusually generous captain. It is not up to the umpire to determine why the fielding captain wants to withdraw an appeal. That is his prerogative. By the same token, the umpire can refuse to accept the withdrawal and his decision is final. As umpire, you can take into consideration the circumstances. If, for instance, there were only three or four balls remaining and 100 runs to win, the batting side cannot win. Thus, you would comply. This is within the laws of the game. Cricket is a game of great traditions and this is one of them. The important thing is that no law was broken, nor was the game brought into disrepute.

131 Not out. The bail might have fallen back into the groove on the wicket if the wicketkeeper had not caught it.

132 Yes, you should insist that the mask be removed. Masks are not allowed to be worn on the field of play. Umpires and scorers must be able to recognise everyone on the field of play. As an umpire, you must be able to see that only nominated players are taking part and that no batsman is batting for a second time.

Page 64 Matt Price

133 Immediately call and signal no ball, because a beamer is an illegal delivery. If you think it was accidentally bowled, give the bowler a first and final warning. If you believe it was deliberately bowled, have the bowler removed from bowling again in that innings, report the bowler and award five penalty runs to the batting side.

134 Do nothing. The ball did not strike the wicket so there was no obstruction.

135 The striker's end umpire should give the top-order batsman out 'run out'. Even though the wicket at the bowler's end was broken, there was no appeal.

136 If, in the umpire's opinion, the movement of the close fielder distracted the striker, call and signal dead ball. The delivery will not count and must be bowled again.

137 I would be delighted to have someone standing with me to share the decision-making. Because he is not an official umpire, I would agree with him and both captains that he stands only at the striker's end, and that I would stand at the bowler's end. There are fewer decisions to be made at the striker's end whereas the bowler's end umpire has many responsibilities and pressures.

138 No. A boundary six can only come off the striker's bat. This would be four leg byes because the striker was taking evasive action.

139 The batsman is wrong. The removal of the remaining bail is enough to enable a run out. It is when both bails have been removed from the top of the stumps that a stump must be struck out of the ground with the ball or pulled out with the ball in that hand.

140 No. If all the stumps are lying on the ground, one stump can be replaced and either struck out with the ball, or pulled out with the hand holding the ball.

141 Umpires have a duty of care to players and themselves. The protruding tree stump poses a threat of injury to those on the field, so have the area roped off in the interests of safety.

142 No runs are scored. The bowler's end umpire should allow the batsman to complete one run only. This gives the fielding side the chance to try for a run out. As soon as one run has been completed, call and signal dead ball and return both batsmen to their original ends.

143 The fitness of ground, light and weather are the sole responsibility of the umpires. The captains may have their opinions, but they do not matter. So the match must start. If a captain refuses to play, he should be told that such a refusal will result in the match being awarded to the opposing team.

144 If you, the umpire, believe that the non-striker intentionally prevented a fielder from making a catch, the striker should be given out 'caught'. In addition, the non-striker should be reported for obstructing the field. If the act of catching is deemed to be accidental, call and signal dead ball.

Page 68

145 Your verdict must be out 'caught' on appeal. The ball is still live when he hits it a second time. If it had not been caught, no runs could have been scored from the second strike.

146 According to a recent change to the laws, the substitute fielder can keep wicket as long as both captains agree.

147 Call and signal dead ball as soon as the striker places his sweater on the ground. Only a member of the fielding side may place a helmet on the ground, behind the wicketkeeper. No runs can be scored.

Page 69

148 You should call and signal dead ball as soon as the bowler seems to have lost his footing. The striker would have been distracted and is not out.

149 The correct call is to give the non-striker out 'run out'.

150 If the sweatband is on the bowler's bowling arm and in your opinion is causing a distraction, instruct his captain to tell him to remove the offending item of clothing.

Page 70 Suresh Raina

151 Only if the bat fell close to the ball would I consider the bowler to be distracted. If this is the case, give the striker 'out for obstruction' as he had no right to throw his bat.

152 You must send the extra fielder off and continue the match. This is the same situation as if the umpire had miscounted the balls in an over. As soon as he realises the mistake, he must try to ensure that it is not repeated. It cannot be corrected in retrospect.

A similar thing happened in a Test match at Headingley in the mid-1980s between England and India. With the visitors fielding, there was a period of play when some players went off and on the field. Suddenly, it was realised that there were 12 fielders on the ground. The umpires stopped the match, sent the extra fielder off and carried on.

153 Neither umpire has the authority or right to question his colleague's decision or style of umpiring. In any event, this decision is one for the bowler's end umpire. The appropriate action would be to take the square-leg umpire to one side and, out of earshot of the players, quietly but firmly explain the position.

Page 71

154 As the bowler walks back the ball is dead and it could be argued that no distraction is being caused. However, cricket is a game of tradition, and fielders tossing objects around like this is not the norm. So you should speak to your fellow umpire and approach the fielding captain to instruct his fielders to desist from this unorthodox practice.

155 If you believe that the bowler is not giving the batsmen enough time to be ready to receive the next ball, call dead ball and instruct the fielding captain to tell his bowler that the batsmen must be allowed more time. But if you are of the opinion that the batsmen were wasting time deliberately, you should tell them to speed up. Batsmen should be ready to face when the bowler is ready, but this is an unusual situation because the bowler's run up is abnormally short.

156 There is nothing against the laws or the spirit of cricket in the fielder's very exuberant celebration of the catch. The batsmen should be told to focus on their own game and ignore the fielder.

Page 72

157 You must stick with your decision, which was made on the basis of what you have seen. The showing of the bat or refusal to leave the crease is dissent and will result in the batsman being reported to the relevant authorities. In any event, the ball – even a new one – does not always leave a mark on the bat.

158 Out. This is comparable to the switch hit when it was first played, and that is not illegal to this day. There is no law that compels a bowler to run up facing forwards. Opponents will soon get used to this unusual approach.

159 Out 'bowled', on appeal. As the umpire, you have a duty of care to players and seeing a player struggling due to the heat, you should have stopped the game to find out what was wrong. In this case, the striker did not complain and neither did you stop the game, so he is out.

Page 73

160 Not out. The wicket must either be rebuilt then legally broken or one stump replaced in the ground and struck out by the ball or pulled out while ensuring that the hand that touches the stump is holding the ball.

161 It is up to the umpire to decide if the striker was distracted when the cap fell from the bowler's head. Normally, the striker will pull away if he is distracted and the umpire will call and signal dead ball. The fact that the striker did not pull away nor did the umpire call dead ball suggests that there was no distraction. The striker is out on appeal.

162 You have no authority to order the striker to desist from passing wind, so it is in the keeper's best interest to take a few paces back. An unusual situation!

Page 74

163 Out 'bowled' on appeal. There is nothing distracting about a bowler tossing the ball from hand to hand as he approaches the wicket. A spinner is more likely to do this as his approach to the wicket is slow and measured, as opposed to a fast bowler, whose run up is much faster.

164 You must give out 'hit wicket' on appeal. According to the laws, if in attempting to play or playing a legal delivery any part of a striker's person or equipment breaks the wicket, he is out.

165 No, you cannot award a boundary four. No runs can be scored from a deliberate second strike. A second strike is permissible only in defence of the wicket, as long as in so doing the batsman does not prevent a catch from being taken.

Page 75

166 As the umpire, you alone can rule if the tape on the repaired bat is too thick. Bats repaired with tape are a common sight in cricket matches at all levels.

167 You should add the five penalty runs to the fielding team's first innings total. If the team have not already batted, those runs should be added when they eventually start their innings.

168 In any match played under the MCC laws, it is mandatory to toss to determine who bats or fields.

Page 76 Joe Root

169 The batsman is not out. Once both bails have been removed from the top of the wicket, a stump must be struck out of the ground by the ball. Alternatively, a fielder may knock a stump out of the ground with his arm as long as the ball is in that hand. He can also pull the stump out with the hand holding the ball.

I once had an incident in a county match between Glamorgan and Northamptonshire. Jason Brown of Northamptonshire bowled a delivery that was driven back hard to him. It hit his hand, broke the wicket, and both bails fell to the ground. The ball ricocheted into the outfield and the batsmen went for a run. The ball was thrown to the bowler's end where I was standing. With both batsmen in the middle of the pitch, Brown caught the ball in his left hand, pulled a stump out with his right hand, and appealed. I called not out and by the time someone told Brown to remove a stump with the hand holding the ball, the batsman made good his ground.

170 The striker is not out. Under the MCC laws a high bouncer is a no ball, not a wide, so the umpire is wrong to call wide. You should revoke the wide and call and signal no ball.

171 You should have called no ball immediately followed by dead ball. The striker had no right to hit the ball. In any event, the batsman is not out because he cannot be caught off a ball that is lying on the ground.

Page 77

172 Not out. The injured striker can only be run out at the wicketkeeper's end. As the ball was still live, it should have been thrown to the keeper's end for a run out if the injured striker had not regained his ground.

173 Yes, you should check to make sure that the bowler is not causing avoidable damage to the ball by rubbing it on a rough seam on his shirt. It is normal for fielders to try to shine the ball on a smooth, soft area of clothing.

174 Yes. The wearing of a motorcycle helmet is not against the laws. It would only be prohibited if both umpires feel that that type of headgear gives him an unfair advantage or somehow would cause damage to the ball. It is the umpires, not players, who are responsible for fair and unfair play.

Page 78

175 Call no ball and give the striker not out. The bowler must inform the bowler's end umpire whenever he changes hands or goes over or around the wicket. The striker has no similar obligation to inform the umpire of a change in stance.

176 Despite the batsman's claims, if you know that you did not say anything, give him out 'bowled'. This may be a ploy on his part to avoid dismissal.

177 Cricket is a game that is played to 42 laws. It is also a game of longstanding traditions, and players do not traditionally wear shorts on the field of play. But, because village cricket is friendly cricket, players often make up their own rules as they go along. And this is a case in point. In this case you would grant permission for shorts to be worn.

Page 79

178 Remove the bails, shake off the butterfly, then replace the bails and restart play. There is no need to hold up the game.

179 Give the striker out 'for obstruction'. He could not have been out 'bowled' when he made the second strike because the close-in fielder had touched the ball. This is simply a case of a striker hitting the ball when he should not have done so and should therefore lose his wicket.

180 If you believe that the batsmen are wasting time, consult your colleague, then give the batsmen a first and final warning for time wasting. Should there be a repeat, award 5 penalty runs to the fielding team.

The opposite scenario can also arise. If a fielding side are blatantly wasting time to gain an advantage, the umpire can award the batting side.

Page 80

181 The striker is out 'stumped' as the ball is not dead. He cannot be run out as he is not attempting a run.

182 You must rule not out. The striker is not going for a run, so cannot be run out off a no ball. He is merely standing out of his crease.

183 You cannot give the striker out. He was in his ground and only stepped out to avoid being injured by a wild throw from the fielder.

Page 81 Jacques Kallis

184 Not out. It was the batsman not the ball that broke the wicket.

185 Although the umpire's decision is final and he can stick with it, if you make a mistake you can change your mind. In this situation, it would be advisable to quickly call and signal no ball, speak with the scorers, and reinstate the striker. It is important to retain the respect of players, and admitting when you have made a mistake helps.

186 Give the non-striker out 'for obstruction'. There was no lawful reason for him to break the wicket. Award five penalty runs to the fielding side. Cancel the run and return the striker to the other end. The ball will not count in the over and report the offender.

Page 82 Ishant Sharma

187 Under the laws of cricket, he can do so when the bowler's arm is in the delivery swing. In other words, just before the ball leaves his hand.

188 You must give the star batsman out 'run out'. The fielding side do not have to appeal for a catch before going for the run out and they clearly did not.

189 Award a boundary four. The fielder crashed into the boundary board while getting his hand to the ball. He is therefore touching the board with the ball in his hand.

Page 83

190 There is nothing in the laws that specifies what drink players consume on the field. I once umpired a county match at Hove when the home captain ordered a mixture of alcoholic drinks for his players on the field. They all sat down in front of the committee room and drank their drinks as a protest over an issue with the committee.

191 Because this is a deliberate no ball, you immediately call and signal no ball. Instruct the fielding captain to remove the bowler from the attack for the remainder of the innings. The over must be completed by a bowler who did not bowl the previous over and is not due to bowl the next over. After the game, report the offending bowler to the relevant authorities.

192 This is a storm in a tea cup. Umpires do not earmark special pieces of cloth for drying the ball, and if the cloth gets wet, fielders are free to change it. As an umpire, your main concern is that nothing is done by the players to damage or change the condition of the ball.

Page 84

193 Because the striker had touched the ball, it would be fair to call and signal dead ball, cancel the run and return both batsmen to their original ends. On appeal, the striker should be given out 'for obstruction'.

194 You or your fellow umpire should immediately call and signal dead ball so nothing further can happen.

195 If in your opinion the striker had deliberately hit the ball after it had come off his boot, no runs would be scored and, on appeal, he should be given out 'for obstruction'. Once the ball had come off his bat or boot, he had no right to deliberately strike it again.

Page 85

196 No. The player can leave the field and have a substitute, but he cannot leave and return repeatedly.

197 You and your fellow umpire are the sole judges of fair and unfair play. If in your opinion, the appealing is excessive or intimidatory, then you must deal with it. Stop the game and speak to the fielding captain, telling him that the keeper's constant appealing is excessive and intimidatory and must cease immediately. Failure to do so will result in a report and a possible sending off.

198 Out 'bowled', on appeal. The bail does not need to fall to the ground to be considered 'removed'. It needs only to be dislodged from the groove on top of the stumps.

Page 86

199 This sounds like a prime example of time wasting by the bowler. Give a first friendly warning. But if there is a repeat of this behaviour, give an official final warning for time wasting. If there is any further repeat, award five penalty runs to the batting side and ban the bowler from bowling for the rest of the innings. He should also be reported.

200 You cannot take any action unless you are certain you heard the frustrated bowler make a derogatory comment about your umpiring. You may judge it appropriate to give the player a friendly warning to let him know that you will not tolerate any provocative comments from him.

201 No. As soon as the ball misses the wicket, call and signal dead ball so that nothing else can happen. Return the batsmen to their original ends. The ball does not count.

Page 87 Joe Root

202 Yes, you must intervene. Once the toss for innings has been completed, the ground becomes the responsibility of both umpires. They alone determine who enters the field of play. The notion of batsmen being driven to the crease is completely against the traditions of the game. What's more, there is a real chance that the tyres of the car will damage the square and outfield. Sponsorship provides vital lifeblood for the survival of clubs at every level, but batsmen being driven to the crease is a gimmick that would tarnish the image of the game and would not be permitted by the umpires.

203 No boundary six has been scored but there has been illegal fielding. Award five penalty points to the batting side, plus any runs completed.

204 Under the laws of the game, there are no reviews and the umpire's decision is final. The captain has no right to challenge the umpire's decision and should be given a Level 1 warning for dissent.

Page 88 Peter Siddle

205 Before the match started, you should have inspected the ball to be used and instructed the captain to remove any non-standard writing from it. If you had failed to notice the writing before the match, you should now order a change of ball for a standard one.

206 The batsman is not out and can resume his innings. He left his ground under the misapprehension that he had been caught.

A similar thing happened in a Test match in the Caribbean several years ago, but the umpires got it wrong. A batsman miss-hit a full pitch, which was caught. Not hearing the no ball call, he left his ground, heading for the pavilion. The fielder quickly broke the wicket at the keeper's end and the batsman was given out 'run out'. As soon as the batsman had left his ground, one of the umpires should have called and signalled dead ball so nothing else could happen.

207 The incoming batsman has three minutes to take strike or for his colleague to do so. If he exceeds that time, on appeal, you must give him out 'timed out'.

Page 89

208 Immediately call and signal dead ball. The fielder's aggression is dangerous and unacceptable. After consultation with your fellow umpire, tell the fielding captain to send his angry fielder off for a Level 3 offence. A new law allows umpires to send a player off the field for poor behaviour. You should also report him.

209 Immediately the dog picks the ball up, call and signal dead ball. Consult your colleague and decide how many runs to award. If you felt that a boundary would have been scored, signal four.

210 The fielding captain cannot use the match ball. He also cannot practice on any part of the pitch or square.

Page 90

211 This is clearly a case of deliberate time wasting. Give the fielding captain a first and final warning. If the time wasting continues, call and signal dead ball. Award five penalty runs to the batting side and inform the captain that the bowler is banned for the rest of the innings. Report the offending player. See page 142, question 180.

212 No. The law has been changed. Once the captain who won the toss has informed his opposite and the umpires of his decision, he cannot change his mind.

213 You can recall both teams to resume the game if playing time remains. You can prevent this kind of situation developing by checking the scoreboard continually and, if necessary, ensuring the score is corrected. In particular, before the start of the final over, it is important to check with the scorers that the board is correct and to count every run as it is scored.

Page 91

214 This could merely be a ploy by the fielding captain to save face after dropping two catches. The bowler did not seem to have any problems gripping and controlling the ball, so it cannot have been overly slippery. The safest course of action would be to consult your fellow umpire before making a final decision.

215 As long as you are satisfied that the short run was not intentional, award one run.

216 The away captain is right. If the ball touches any part of the boundary rope, line or fence, then it counts as a boundary. You should remind both captains that the umpires alone will decide where the boundary lies.

Page 92

217 Award five runs to the batsman. The boundary four is the minimum award and you can add the additional single run.

218 No ball takes precedence over a wide ball, so you should award just one run to the batting team.

219 Award one run for the wide ball, then call and signal dead ball. No runs can be scored or wickets taken.

Page 93 Graeme Smith

220 Give the striker out 'bowled'. The non-striker cannot be run out because the ball was not touched by a fielder.

221 The correct decision is to give out 'hit wicket'.

222 Your ruling should be out 'caught' out on appeal.

Page 94 Steve Smith

223 Not out. The ball has been played onto the ground from the first strike, so the batsman cannot be caught. If the ball had not made contact with the ground and it had been caught and held, he would have been out 'caught' after the second strike.

224 You cannot give the batsman out. The game is played on top of the grass, so the grass is the ground. The fact that some blades of grass were longer than the others makes no difference.

225 Not out. For you to give out, the batsman must have played the ball directly onto his wicket or it must have come off his person.

Page 95

226 Award a boundary four to the striker if the ball touched the ground, or a boundary six if it went full over the boundary.

227 The fielder can leave the field of play but he cannot have a substitute because he was not injured.

228 Not out on appeal. As soon as the branch of the tree fell off, you should call and signal dead ball. If you thought a boundary would have been scored, award four runs. If not, award the runs completed.

Page 96

229 Yes, the one run will count. Some scorers try to tell umpires that they have miscounted, but they have no authority to do so. Right or wrong, the umpire's decision is final.

230 Out 'hit wicket'. The batsman's gesturing with the bat is unnecessary. Only scorers need to acknowledge umpires' signals.

231 Your decision must be out 'run out' because the final throw removed the stump from the ground, with the batsman short of his ground.

Page 97

232 Not out. The law says that some part of the batsman's person or bat must be grounded behind the popping crease, as in this instance.

233 You cannot give the batsman out. The runner has not moved to obstruct the fielder. He is entitled to remain where he stood.

234 Time wasting comes under the law on unfair play of which you, the umpire – together with your colleague – are the sole judges. No player can lawfully challenge you on this. In this case, you and your fellow umpire should confer and decide whether to give the captain a Level 1 or Level 2 charge. If he continues to be aggressive, a Level 4 charge could be given and he should be instructed to take himself off the field. Should he fail to obey, he would be told that a failure to comply with the umpires' instruction would ultimately result in his team forfeiting the match. The captain would also be reported.

Page 98

235 The batsman is out 'caught'. At no time did the ball touch the ground. This is a situation where both umpires would have to confer because the striker's end umpire would more likely be in a better position to see if the ball touched the ground than his colleague.

236 There is nothing in the laws governing this state of affairs. Umpires have a duty to conduct themselves in a manner that does not bring the game into disrepute, and smelling of alcohol demeans the game. LBWs are a matter of opinion and the umpire is always in the best position to make that judgement. Nevertheless, a report should be sent to the league executive.

237 Immediately call and signal dead ball to prevent a run out from happening. You should consult your fellow umpire to decide how many runs would have been scored had there been no intervention and award them to the batting side. It's worth noting that prior to the start of the match, you should have told the captains what would happen if a person or animal enters the field of play and makes contact with the ball while it is in play.

Page 99

238 Unless there is a playing regulation banning advertising, you must allow the player to use his colourful bat. The laws of the game define only the size of the bat and the requirement to ensure that it does not cause avoidable damage to the ball.

239 If you are convinced that the captain's claim is correct, you should tell the fielding captain to instruct the bowler to remove the watch.

240 The law is clear; if there are three minutes or more of playing time left, the over must be completed by a fielder who did not bowl the previous over and who is not due to bowl the next.

Page 100

241 Yes. Any member of his team can attend the toss. At least one umpire must supervise the toss, and at this time inform both captains on the standards of behaviour expected from them and their teams during the match.

242 You should summon the offending player's captain and issue a Level 1 offence to that player. He should also be reported to the relevant authority.

243 The batsman is run out because he had initially set off for a run. He cannot be stumped from a ball which had been thrown by a fielder.

Page 101 Jimmy Anderson

244 Out 'caught'. The non-striker and umpires are part of play, so if a ball that has been played strikes any part of their body, clothing or equipment and is caught before hitting the ground, on appeal, you must give out 'caught'.

245 Your must give out 'caught' on appeal. It is routine to see players with taped fingers and this does not give that player an unfair advantage. The opposing captain has no right of appeal.

246 The player is out. The boundary rope should have been replaced in its original position, but as it was not, the boundary line has changed. It was your duty and that of your colleague to ensure that the rope was put back in its original position. This is a bad mistake, but when the umpires do not check to make sure that the boundary rope is in its proper position, they effectively accept the changed boundary.

Page 102

247 Once the umpires have agreed with the scorers on the result, that decision will stand. If that were not the case, there is the theoretical possibility that a scorer could change the score when he was on his own. Umpires should tell scorers to cross check with each other as the game progresses so as to prevent this situation from arising.

248 You cannot permit this. The law states clearly that judgements on the fitness of ground, weather and light are the sole responsibility of the umpires. They will do inspections on their own and report to the captains afterwards.

249 There is no problem giving the bowler a reply as long as he is not disrespectful.

In 1989, I umpired a One-Day International between Pakistan and the West Indies in India. Pakistan's first change bowler at my end was their great leg spinner Abdul Qadir. Off the first delivery, the West Indian batsman Richie Richardson tried to sweep the ball, but it deflected off his pad and ran to fine leg. The batsmen ran three. As I signalled leg byes, Qadir said to me in annoyance, 'Mr Umpire, he did not play a shot'. My reply to him was 'I do not tell you how to bowl, so do not tell me how to umpire'. After that, he gave me no further advice.

Page 103   Ben Stokes

250 You can allow the wicketkeeper to remove his pads and gloves and act purely as a fielder. According to the laws, it is not compulsory for the fielding team to have a wicketkeeper.

251 Consult your colleague and if you agree that the flapping sleeve caused distraction, call and signal dead ball, give the striker not out and tell the bowler to bowl that ball again.

252 Give the striker out 'for obstruction'. Although the delivery was a no ball and he would not have been out 'bowled', the ball is still live and the batsman has no right to deliberately touch it, unless permission to do so by a member of the fielding side has been given.

Page 104

253 You should immediately call and signal no ball. Despite the bowler's seeming apology, instruct the fielding captain to remove the bowler from the attack for the remainder of the innings. The over must be completed by someone who did not bowl the previous over, and who is not due to bowl the next one. The bowler should be reported to the relevant authorities for dangerous and unfair bowling.

254 Yes, he has. From the time of the toss, the ground is under the umpires' control. The groundsman has no authority to take initiative in such matters without the permission or instruction of the umpires.

255 Not out. You cannot give the striker out 'hit wicket' off a no ball.

Page 105

256 It cannot be a wide if the batsman strikes it. Always wait till the ball has gone past the striker before you call wide. In this situation, award four runs to the striker.

257 Give the non-striker out because he left his ground before the wicketkeeper broke the stumps. This situation arises frequently in cricket when there is a mix up between batsmen running between the wickets with wickets in hand and a tail-ender batting with a top order batsman. In order to give his team a better chance of winning the game or making a big total, the tail-ender will generally walk off and sacrifice his wicket rather than allow the top order batsman to leave the field.

258 No, absolutely not. In my 27 years of umpiring there were numerous times when I would have given a batsman out but nobody appealed. One memorable instance was in 1982 when I umpired a match between Cambridge University and Leicestershire at Fenners. David Gower of Leicester was in full flow, batting stylishly to the frustration of the Cambridge bowlers. He missed a middle stump half volley, which struck him on the pad but there was no appeal and he carried on with his devastating innings. During the next over, Gower was at the non-striker's end and asked me if I would have given him out 'LBW' if there had been an appeal, to which I said, yes. With a wry smile he said 'I thought it was close'.

Page 106 Graeme Swann

259 The striker cannot be given out 'LBW' if the ball has hit the bat. But you cannot assume that the ball has hit the bat just because you heard a noise. Don't guess; if you are uncertain rule not out.

260 You and your fellow umpire are solely responsible for the fitness of ground, weather and light. In October 2010 the law was changed to give the umpires sole responsibility for ruling on the fitness of the ground for play. Captains are not consulted, nor are they allowed to accompany the umpires on inspections. They can do their own inspections but the umpires will tell them when they think it is fit to play.

Prior to the rule change, I had to deal with a similar situation in a county match between Middlesex and Somerset at Lords in 1983. With Middlesex fielding in Somerset's second innings on day two, just after tea there was a huge thunderstorm. By the time the ground staff had succeeded in covering the pitch with a tarpaulin, the ground was wet and play had to be abandoned for the day.

Next morning we had bright sunshine but two strips of the pitch were still very wet. The conditions were ideal for the two Middlesex spinners Phil Edmonds and John Emburey even though the Somerset had the mighty Viv Richards at the crease and their captain Ian Botham still to bat.

Mike Gatting, the Middlesex captain, repeatedly urged my colleague and I to allow play to start, saying that he would take responsibility if any player got injured on the unfit patches. It wasn't until after lunch, when the ground was drying out, that my colleague and I decided that the match could be restarted. Botham was furious with us, saying that it would not be fit to start so early. We ignored him and stuck to our guns. Play started and very quickly Edmonds and Emburey skittled Richards, Botham and the rest of the Somerset batsmen cheaply, leaving Middlesex in need of only 140 runs to win. Botham was furious, but Somerset then bowled out Middlesex for around 120 and won the match. Botham was ecstatic with the result.

261 The opening batsman is out 'run out', because he is closest to the wicket that was broken. The catch was not taken.

Page 107

262 As soon as the boot strikes the ball, call and signal dead ball. Award five penalty runs to the batting side. The ball does not count, so scores are tied with one ball remaining. Report the offence.

263 It all depends on whether you thought the ball was dead or not. Did the fielding side look as if they were not planning to try for a wicket or was it clear that the batsmen was not looking to try for another run? You must make your decision based on what you have seen.

264 Give the batsman out 'for obstructing the field'. The batsman has no right to touch the ball, unless to protect himself or to defend his wicket, as long as he does not prevent a catch being taken. The batsman can handle the ball only with permission from a member of the fielding side.

In 1989 I umpired in the Test series between Pakistan and India. In the closing stages of the first test in Karachi, Pakistan were batting out time as the match looked to be ending in a tame draw. India's fast bowler Viveck Razdan bowled to Salim Malik, who played the ball defensively, then picked it up and lobbed it to the gully fielder. Had there been an appeal, I would have had no option but to give him out 'for handling the ball'. However, there was no appeal.

Page 108

265 There is no restriction on where the keeper can stand to receive a throw from the outfield. If the batsman is not in his ground, he must be given out 'run out' on appeal.

266 Neither captain has the authority to make such decisions or demands. Before the toss, the pitch is the responsibility of the groundsman. After the toss, the umpires take charge. A captain can say that he does not want the pitch rolled before his team bat and say which roller to use if there is a choice, but that is all.

267 This depends on the precise timing of the appeal. There can be an appeal before the bowler starts his run up for the start of the next over, but not after the call of time prior to an interval or close of play.

Page 109

268 Give out 'for obstructing the field'. The striker can only hit or touch the ball a second time to protect himself from injury, to defend his wicket, or if a member of the fielding side gives permission to do so.

269 The away captain is correct. In this case the threshold is 75. One of the duties of the umpires before the match starts is to clarify the playing regulations for the match with both captains prior to the toss, including guidance about enforcing the follow on.

270 Not out. You must give the batsman the benefit of the doubt. To give out, you must be absolutely certain that the ball did not first hit the bat or the glove holding the bat before the pad or part of his person.

Page 110   Sachin Tendulkar

271 Not out. This is blatantly unfair play – a desperate attempt to get a wicket. You should also give the wicketkeeper a first and final warning.

272 You should immediately call and signal dead ball. No wicket can result and no runs can be scored. It's worth remembering that the umpire's pre-match duties include informing both captains what will happen if a person or animal comes onto the field of play and touches the live ball.

273 The incoming batsman is not out. With the umpires wrongly getting into an argument with the dismissed striker, the game has come to a stop. It would be ridiculous to then allow the incoming batsman to be timed out. You should have curtailed this exchange at the start. It's a good rule to avoid this kind of conversation with any player. The argumentative batsman should have been told that a refusal to leave the field of play would ultimately result in his team forfeiting the match. He could be reported for dissent.

Page 111

274 You have no authority to stop the bowler changing ends, but if in your opinion he is deliberately wasting time, you can give him a first and final warning. If he offends again, award five penalty runs to the fielding side and ban the bowler from bowling for the remainder of the innings. You would also report the player for the offence. Umpires should be proactive in cases like this and not wait for an opponent to complain.

275 Award four runs to the batting side. Short runs do not come into play when a boundary is scored.

276 As long as he asked you politely, there is no reason not to pass the ball to the bowler. You are in no way giving the team an unfair advantage. An important part of being a good umpire is maintaining the respect of players. If you treat them courteously, they are likely to reciprocate.

Page 112

277 As soon as the striker falls, the bowler's end umpire should call and signal dead ball. That ball will not count and will be re-bowled.

278 Give out 'LBW' on appeal. There is no specified time in which the umpire can deliberate before making his decision. Furthermore, neither may a batsman refer a decision to the third umpire unless, as in this case, it was a televised match with a special playing regulation that allows that challenge.

279 The striker is out 'caught' on appeal. If in the umpire's opinion the fielder had control of the ball and of his further movement, the catch is legal. If the juggle was completely under control, not only could the fielder have finally caught the ball, he was also in control of his further movement, in that after deliberately tossing the ball up several times, he eventually allowed it to fall to the ground.

Page 113

280 You cannot give a batsman out unless there is an appeal, so in this instance, you should do nothing. Under the laws of cricket, even if a batsman is clean bowled, he can remain at the crease if there is no appeal.

281 There is nothing in the laws to prevent a player from smoking on the field. Cricket is a game of great traditions, and traditionally players do not smoke on the field of play. In this case, you could speak with the player and his captain along these lines. If the player continues to smoke, let the game go on, but report the incident to the relevant authorities.

282 This is potentially a case of dangerous and unfair bowling. If, taking into account the skill of the batsman, you think the bowling by its length, height and direction is dangerous and unfair, call no ball and give the bowler a warning. Should he persist with this type of bowling, you may ultimately be obliged to ban him from bowling for the rest of the innings.

Many years ago I was banned from bowling in a county match playing for Hampshire against Worcester at Portsmouth. Worcester's Alan Ormrod scored a century, frequently playing at me, edging through slips and making an occasional good stroke. In frustration, I bowled him two successive bouncers, the second of which struck him on the head and he fell to the ground. When he eventually took strike again, I immediately let rip another bouncer, which flew past his head to the wicketkeeper. Without warning, the umpire spoke to my captain and I was banned from bowling for the rest of the innings. In those days the umpire's decision was respected as final and players did not challenge them, unlike today.

Page 114 Stuart Broad

283 The non-striker is out 'run out'. Even though the striker originally left his ground, he regained it before the non-striker joined him, so he cannot be run out.

284 This is a decision for the striker's end umpire. It was his duty to ensure the wicket was properly re-made after it was broken. It is quite possible that the bail fell off after the LBW decision was given, so the decision stands.

285 It is obvious that the striker was distracted here, and his objection is valid. Immediately call and signal dead ball and make sure that the ball doesn't count in that over. The batsman is not out. Ensure that all players and officials immediately leave the field of play.

Page 115 Joe Root

286 As soon as it is obvious that the fielder is injured, you should call and signal dead ball so no further action can take place. Award the striker the number of runs he completed before the injury.

287 Not out. Like a cap, a wig is meant to be worn on the player's head, not on the ground. This ruling applies even if, as in this case, it fell off by accident.

288 Immediately call and signal dead ball. The ringing of the phone was not intentional so there was no obstruction. The ball cannot count in the over.

Page 116

289 If the behaviour of the spectators is so toxic that it is affecting the game, you could ask both captains to make an appeal to the crowd to treat the umpires with respect, or they will walk off the field.

I had a similar experience in 1989 while umpiring a Test match in Pakistan between Pakistan and India. India were fielding in front of 30,000 noisy spectators. Suddenly, stones were thrown onto the field near to the boundary where Sanjay Manjrekar and Sachin Tendulkar were fielding. Their captain threatened to take his players off for their safety. My fellow umpire and I asked the authorities to take action. An appeal was made over the loudspeaker to treat the visitors with respect and the game resumed without further incident.

290 This is one of the recent changes to the laws. As long as the next batsman has not begun his innings, the other batsman can be recalled.

291 The striker has no right to touch the ball with the hand not on the bat other, except in self defence. Even though this striker walked down the pitch holding the ball, I would call dead ball and give him not out.

I once saw Mark Ramprakash catch a ball while he was batting. He had played the ball to a close fielder and was standing in his ground. Suddenly, the fielder hurled the ball straight at Ramprakash, who caught it and threw it to the ground. Ramprakash, clearly not amused, gave the errant fielder a glare and the game continued. He was within his rights to catch the ball.

Page 117

292 You would have felt the sudden gust and seen the batsman recoil as the cap lifts from his head, so you should immediately call and signal dead ball to prevent any further development. The striker is not out.

293 When the assaulted umpire has recovered, he and his colleague must summon the fielding captain. The captain will be instructed to send the offending bowler off the field for the remainder of the match. The abusive fielder will be given a Level 2 disciplinary breach and five penalty runs will be awarded to the batting side. The fielding captain will be told that any Level 1 breach by any member of his team will immediately result in penalty runs. It will be reported.

294 You cannot give the batsman out. He made his ground, so he can jump in the air afterwards. What's more, the ball is still live and further runs could be scored from the throw.

Page 118 Misbah-ul-Haq

295 The striker's end umpire should give the striker out 'run out'. The umpire should also call and signal no ball.

296 You should inspect the ball, but unless you or your colleague witnessed the alleged tampering by the spectator, there is nothing further you can do. If there is obvious damage to the ball, replace it with one of similar condition. The dismissal stands.

297 Award nine runs – four to the striker plus five penalty runs for the ball striking the helmet on the ground. Call and signal dead ball as soon as the ball strikes the helmet on the ground. Nothing else can happen.

Page 119 Chris Woakes

298 Immediately call and signal dead ball. Neither the ball nor the wicket count. The match starts when the bowler's end umpire calls play for both batsmen, his colleague and the fielding side to hear. He has not done that so the match has not started.

299 Because the injured batsman cannot continue, he will be retired not out. The match is tied because scores are level and there are no more batsman to continue.

300 Not out. This is because the wicketkeeper deliberately took his glove off and threw it on the ground. Had it accidentally fallen off, the batsman would have been run out on appeal. Award five penalty runs to the batting side.

Index of offences and issues

Use this index to locate the question numbers referring to specific types of cricket offence or issue. Some questions that deal with more than one issue appear more than once.

About the authors

John Holder

The internationally respected umpire John Holder was born in Barbados and started his cricketing career in the island's 1st Division competition. Having moved to the United Kingdom in the 1960s, he trained as a guard on the London Underground. He joined Hampshire County Cricket Club as a fast bowler in 1966 and retired in 1972 due to injury.

After moving to the north of England to play league cricket in Lancashire and Yorkshire, Holder was appointed to the First Class Umpires' Panel in 1983 and umpired for the next 27 years. He made his Test match debut as an umpire in 1988 at Lords and stood in his last Test match there in an Ashes Test in 2001. John and the late John Hampshire were the first pair of neutral umpires when they stood in the Test series between Pakistan and India in 1989. In total, Holder has umpired 11 Tests, 23 One-Day Internationals and several domestic finals.

After retirement as a top-level umpire in 2009, Holder was employed by the International Cricket Council as a regional umpires' performance manager with responsibility for Europe, the Americas and the Caribbean. He stepped down from that role at the end of 2010.

Holder co-authored the first edition of *You Are the Umpire* with Paul Trevillion in 2008. In 2018, he was awarded the Cricket Society's Ian Jackson award for outstanding services to cricket as a player, umpire and author.

Paul Trevillion

A world-famous sports artist, dubbed the 'Leonardo of Line' and the 'Master of Movement', Paul Trevillion has worked with many of the greatest sporting legends of the past 70 years.

In 1952, Trevillion met and drew HRH Prince Philip at the Mansion House Awards. The recognition he received for this commission provided openings for his work in the national press and launched Trevillion's career in cricket illustration with his drawings of the 1953 England and Australian Ashes teams for the *Sporting Record*.

In 1955, Trevillion presented Sir Winston Churchill with his portrait painting of the wartime leader. Churchill was so pleased with the painting, he personally signed it.

Trevillion is the author of more than 20 books that have sold throughout the world. He was the artist behind the 'Gary Player Golf Class', a series that appeared in more than 1,500 newspapers worldwide and became the largest syndicated sports feature in history. Trevillion's illustrations brought to life the 1960s comic-book footballer 'Roy of the Rovers'. He is the creator of the 'You Are the Ref' and 'You Are the Umpire' comic strip conundrums. His artwork has appeared in galleries and museums throughout the world.

Acknowledgements

The MCC Working Party deals with all matters related to the making of the Laws of Cricket. I was a member of that Working Party for three years, in which time my interest and knowledge in the game of cricket increased significantly. I would like to thank the other members of that group from whom I learned so much, including the late Nigel Plews, John Jameson, Sheila Hill and Stan Bennett. I would also like to thank Nigel Tench, Eric Roberts and Dave Whiteman, all ACO instructors on the laws of the game.

Paul Trevillion's ability to depict scenarios with his artwork has been amazing, as has his enthusiasm and love for cricket. He and his wife Lorraine have become good friends of mine. Thanks also to Trevor Davies and Ella Parsons whose professionalism and attention to detail have impressed me hugely.

John Holder

Firstly, I would like to thank my much-valued friend and *You Are the Umpire* other half for his unchallengeable knowledge of the laws of the great game of cricket. John Holder's concise explanation of every umpiring decision in this book has inspired my artist's brush. To Trevor Davies, for his foresight in stressing the need to include the new umpiring laws, to enable the cricket world to understand the new laws more fully. Special thanks to Rick 'THE COLONEL' Mayston, my long-suffering agent and finally, the wonderful editing and expertise of Ella Parsons.

Paul Trevillion